Easy
FISH and SEAFOOD

TORMONT

TORMONT

Graphic design: Zapp
Choice of recipes: Diane Mineau and Marc Maulà
Food preparation/styling: Josée Robitaille
Photographs: Marc Bruneau, Nathalie Dumouchel, Melissa du Fretay, Studio Pol Martin (Ontario) Ltd., Rodrigo Gutiérrez
Props courtesy of the following: Arthur Quentin, Geneviève Lethu, La Maison d'Émilie, Pier 1 Imports, Regal Ware Inc., Stokes
Editor: Isabel Fonte

Pictured on front cover: *Pickerel with Fresh Herbs and Fresh Cod with Tomato Curry*, see page 233
Pictured on back cover: *Tropical Scampi*, see page 53

©2002 Tormont Publications Inc.
338 Saint Antoine Street East, Montreal, Canada H2Y 1A3
Tel. (514) 954-1441 Fax (514) 954-5086
www.tormont.com

Canada

The publisher thanks Heritage Canada for the support awarded under
the Book Publishing Industry Development Program.

Government of Québec—Book Publishing Tax Credit Program—Administered by SODEC

Printed in China

Contents

Introduction

Fish and seafood are remarkable foods. They are very nutritious, easy to prepare, and versatile. As this book will show you, they can be cooked in many different ways and served with a wide variety of accompaniments. Thanks to state-of-the-art conservation techniques and to the speed of transportation, your local fish store can now offer a wide range of fish and seafood from around the world.

Rich in protein and vitamins, fish has tender flesh that is low in calories and easy to digest. Fish is also an excellent source of phosphorous, magnesium, iron and iodine. It can be divided into three categories, according to its fat content: lean fish has less than 5% fat (sole, skate, porgy, etc.), medium-lean fish has between 5% and 10% fat (sardines, salmon, etc.) and oily fish has more than 10% fat (tuna, mackerel, eel, etc.).

As for seafood, it can be divided into two groups: crustaceans (lobster, crab, shrimp, etc.) and mollusks (oysters, mussels, scallops, etc.). All are low in fat and are excellent sources of protein and mineral salts.

Many people are wary of preparing fish and seafood. However, with the background presented in the next few pages, you should feel confident enough to enjoy cooking these delicious foods. The most important factor is to make sure that the products you buy are absolutely fresh. Feel free to ask your fishmonger for advice. Not only will you find help in selecting your fish and seafood, but you may also learn helpful tips on storage, preparation and cooking.

So why not try the easy-to-prepare recipes provided in this book? They will be sure to win over family and guests alike.

Substitution Guide*

Atlantic Salmon	*Pacific Salmon, Salmon Trout*
Black Sea Bass	*Striped Bass, Sea Bass, Red Snapper*
Bluefish	*Bonito, Sea Trout, Pike*
Bonito	*Mackerel, Tuna*
Carp	*Pike, Cod*
Cod	*Haddock, Halibut, Hake, Pike*
Eel	*Conger Eel*
Grouper	*Black Sea Bass, Striped Bass, Gray Mullet*
Gurnard	*Sea Bream, Scorpion Fish, Porgy*
Haddock	*Hake, Plaice, Sole, Turbot*
Halibut	*Cod, Grouper, Turbot*
Herring	*Mackerel, Sprat*
John Dory	*Sole*
Mackerel	*Swordfish, Herring, Tuna*
Monkfish	*Cod, Halibut, Grouper*
Pacific Salmon	*Atlantic Salmon, Salmon Trout*
Pike	*Cod, Whitefish*
Plaice	*Sole, Flounder*
Pompano	*Butterfish, Scabbardfish, Sole*
Porgy	*Sea bream, Scabbardfish*
Rainbow Trout	*Salmon, Salmon Trout*
Red Mullet	*Sea Bream, Gray Mullet, Gurnard*
Red Bream	*Sea Bream, Gilt-Head Bream*
Red Snapper	*Sea Bream, Red Bream, Red Mullet*
Salmon Trout	*Salmon, Rainbow Trout, Char*
Sardine	*Anchovy, Smelt, Small Mackerel*
Sea Bass	*Black Sea Bass, Striped Bass, Red Snapper*
Sea Bream	*Red Mullet, Porgy, Grouper*
Shark	*Swordfish, Sea Bass, Tuna*
Skate	*None*
Smelt	*Anchovy, Small Mackerel, Sardine*
Sole	*Plaice, Pike, Flounder*
Striped Bass	*Black Sea Bass, Sea Bass, Red Snapper*
Swordfish	*Bonito, Sea Bass, Tuna*
Tilefish	*Cod, Striped Bass, Sea Bass*
Sea Trout	*Bluefish, Cod, Haddock*
Tuna	*Bonito, Swordfish*
Turbot	*Cod, Haddock, Plaice, Pompano*

*This guide will help you replace a type of fish that is not readily available where you live, or allow you to vary your menu. Note that these substitutions are suggestions, not perfect equivalents.

Cooking Methods

FISH	smoked	raw[1]	marinated	steamed	poached	braised	fried	sautéed	baked	grilled
Black Sea Bass		•		•	•	•		•	•	•
Bluefish				•	•		•	•	•	•
Bonito		•		•	•			•	•	•
Carp				•	•	•	•	•	•	
Cod				•	•	•	•	•		•
Eel	•			•	•	•		•		•
Grouper		•			•		•	•		•
Gurnard				•	•	•		•		•
Haddock	•		•	•	•	•		•		•
Halibut				•	•	•	•	•		•
Herring			•				•		•	•
John Dory				•	•	•		•	•	•
Mackerel	•		•	•			•	•		•
Monkfish				•	•	•		•		•
Pike				•			•	•	•	
Plaice	•	•		•	•	•		•	•	
Pompano	•					•		•		•
Porgy				•	•	•	•	•		•
Rainbow Trout	•			•				•	•	
Red Bream		•	•	•				•	•	
Red Mullet					•		•	•		•
Red Snapper	•	•		•	•		•	•	•	•
Salmon[2]	•	•	•	•	•			•	•	•
Salmon Trout	•		•	•	•			•		•
Sardine			•				•	•	•	•
Sea Bass	•	•	•	•	•	•				•
Sea Bream		•	•	•				•	•	
Shark					•	•	•	•		•
Skate				•	•			•		•
Smelt							•	•	•	•
Sole		•		•	•	•	•	•		
Striped Bass		•		•	•	•		•		•
Swordfish	•	•				•	•	•		•
Tilefish				•	•	•				
Sea Trout	•			•	•			•		•
Tuna		•	•				•	•		•
Turbot		•		•	•	•	•	•	•	•

[1] Obviously, 'raw' is not a cooking method. However it is worth pointing out which kinds of fish can be prepared as sushi, sashimi, etc.
[2] Atlantic and Pacific salmon.

Cleaning Fish

1

With kitchen scissors, cut off the dorsal fin.

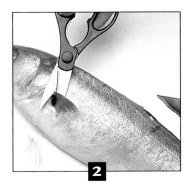

2

Then cut off the other fins.

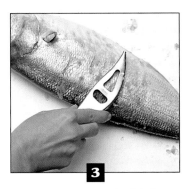

3

With a scaler, scale the fish from the tail up to the head.

4

Or use the blunt side of a knife to scale the fish.

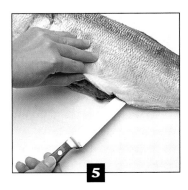

5

Using the point of a knife, cut down the underside of the fish.

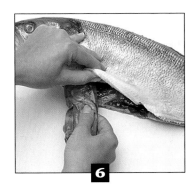

6

Remove the entrails.

7

Wash the inside and outside of the fish thoroughly under cold, running water.

Boning Fish

1

Hold the cleaned fish open and run the blade of a sharp knife between the flesh and the ribs to detach them.

2

With the point of a knife, cut along the backbone on both sides, from the tail towards the head.

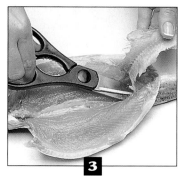

3

Cut through the backbone at the base of the head, then pull it up from the head towards the tail. Cut through the other end at the base of the tail.

Filleting Fish

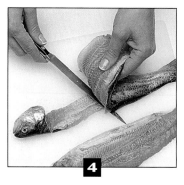

1

Without cutting off the head, cut through the gills of the fish.

2

With the blade of the knife, cut along the backbone from just behind the head to the tail, cutting as close as possible to the bone.

3

Lift the fillet away, sliding the knife between the flesh and the ribs.

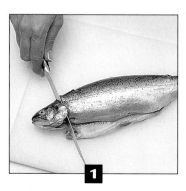

4

Turn the fish over and lift away the other fillet.

5

Slide the blade between the flesh and the ribs and remove the ribs.

6

Remove any remaining small bones with tweezers.

Slicing Fillets

Slice the fillet into 1½-inch (3.5 cm) wide pieces.

Slicing Escalopes

With a sharp knife, cut wide pieces by placing the knife slightly on the diagonal.

Cutting out Steaks

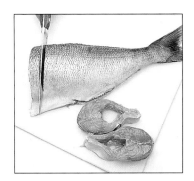

Use a round fish that has been cleaned. Cut off the head, then cut 1-inch (2.5 cm) thick slices.

Preparing Tournedos

1

Remove the backbone from the steak.

2

Remove about 1 inch (2.5 cm) of flesh from the ends.

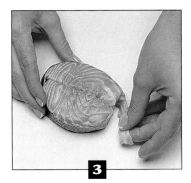

3

Fold the loose skin around the flesh.

4

Tie the steak with string.

Skinning a Flat Fish

1

Cut through the skin just above
the tail of the fish.

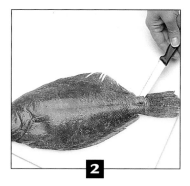

2

Lift the skin with the point of
the knife.

3

Holding the fish firmly by the tail
with a cloth, peel the skin away
from the cut towards the head.
Turn the fish over and repeat.

Boning Sardines

1

Cut off the head.

2

With a knife, cut along the
underside, remove the entrails
and wash the cavity.

3

Slide the knife blade between the
flesh and the ribs, on each side.

4

With the point of the knife,
detach the backbone on both
sides, up to the tail.

5

Pull on the backbone all the way
to the tail and, if necessary, cut
the end with scissors.

Shelling Oysters

1

Wash oysters thoroughly under cold running water.

2

Insert the point of the oyster knife into the hinge, at the narrow end of the oyster. Twist the knife slightly to open the shell.

3

Hold the oyster firmly with a cloth and slide the blade along the inside from one end to the other.

4

With the knife, cut through the connecting muscle to detach the oyster from its shell.

Preparing Shrimp

1

Peel off the shell with your fingers.

2

Cut down the back of the shrimp.

3

Remove the vein.

Cleaning Mussels

Scrub well and debeard mussels by pulling on the byssus (beard) protruding from the shell, then wash under cold water.

Preparing Squid

1

Detach the head and tentacles from the body by holding the tentacles and pulling gently.

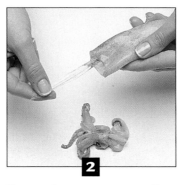

2

Remove the transparent cartilage inside the body, called the quill, and any remaining entrails.

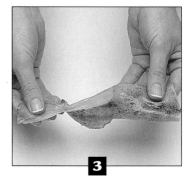

3

Remove the fins.

4

Peel off the skin and wash the body of the squid.

5

Remove the beak and discard.

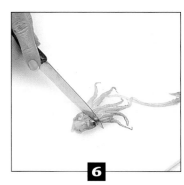

6

Cut eyes from tentacles and discard.

Preparing Lobster

Break the tail section away from the body.

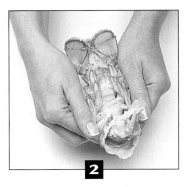

Break the tail open and remove the meat.

Detach the legs by breaking them at the joint.

Separate each claw from the rest of the leg.

Detach the small part of each claw.

With lobster pincers or a nut cracker, break open the claws and remove the meat.

Herbs

Oregano

Bay leaves

Thai basil

Coriander

Chives

Thyme

Mint

Rosemary

Sage

Chervil

Basil

Parsley

Dill

Tarragon

Sorrel

Garlic chives

Spices

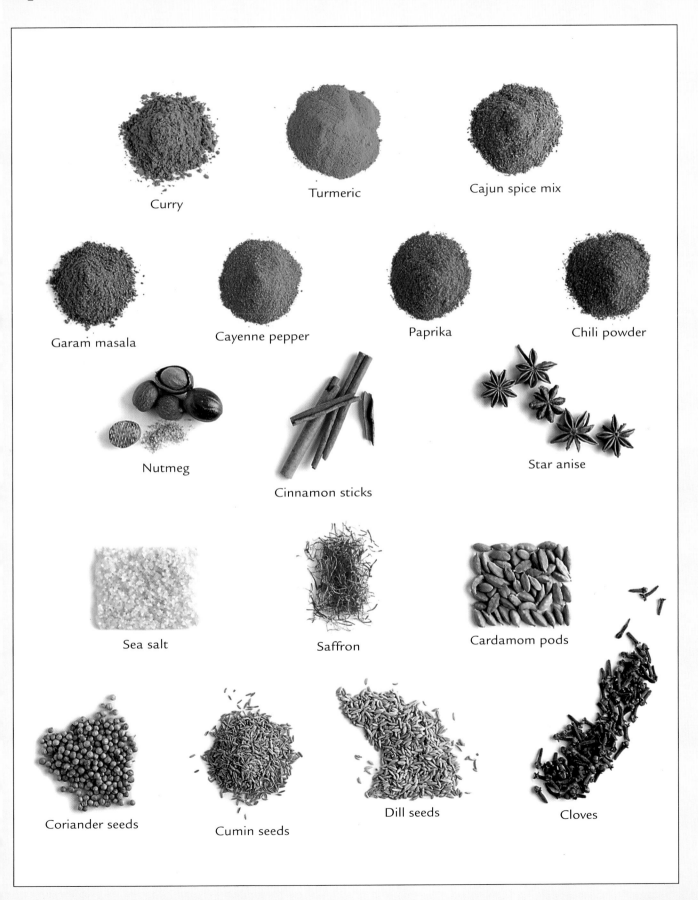

Curry

Turmeric

Cajun spice mix

Garam masala

Cayenne pepper

Paprika

Chili powder

Nutmeg

Cinnamon sticks

Star anise

Sea salt

Saffron

Cardamom pods

Coriander seeds

Cumin seeds

Dill seeds

Cloves

Soups

Fish Stock

(750 ml • 3 cups)

2 lb	fish bones	1 kg
2	onions, chopped	2
2	celery ribs	2
¼ lb	mushrooms, cleaned and sliced	125 g
2	fresh thyme sprigs	2
2	fresh parsley sprigs	2
2	bay leaves	2
	juice of ½ lemon	
	pepper	

- Rinse fish bones under cold running water and place in a large saucepan. Add onions, celery and mushrooms. Cover with water and bring to a boil. Skim and reduce heat to medium.
- Add thyme, parsley, bay leaves, lemon juice and pepper to taste. Cook, uncovered, about 30 minutes. Strain through a sieve lined with cheesecloth.

1 RECIPE

Calories	516	Carbohydrate	52 g
Protein	21 g	Fat	16 g
Fiber	10.8 g		

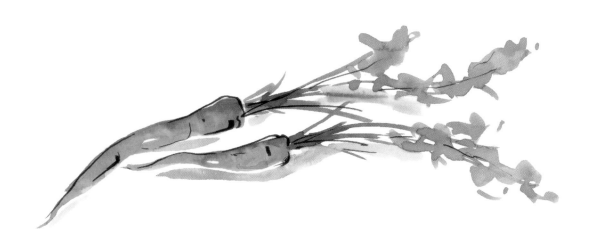

Scallop and Mushroom Soup

(4 to 6 servings)

1	shallot, finely chopped	1
1 lb	fresh scallops, cleaned	500 g
½ lb	fresh mushrooms, cleaned and cut in three	250 g
2	green onions, chopped	2
2	potatoes, peeled and diced small	2
1 cup	dry white wine	250 mL
5 cups	water	1.25 L
½ tsp	fennel seed	2 mL
1 tsp	chopped fresh parsley	5 mL
4 tbsp	butter	60 mL
4 tbsp	all-purpose flour	60 mL
	salt and black pepper	
	cayenne pepper to taste	
	chopped fresh parsley	

- Place shallot, scallops, mushrooms, green onions and potatoes in a saucepan. Pour in wine and water. Add fennel seed, 1 tsp (5 mL) chopped parsley, and season well.

- Bring to a slow boil over medium heat. Scallops will become opaque when cooked. Using a slotted spoon, remove cooked scallops and set aside.

- Continue cooking liquid and vegetables 15 minutes over medium heat, or until potatoes are cooked.

- Heat butter in a sauté pan over medium heat. Sprinkle in flour and mix well; cook 1 minute. Add 2 cups (500 mL) cooking liquid from scallops and whisk to incorporate. Season to taste.

- Pour contents of sauté pan into the saucepan. Whisk liquids to incorporate and cook 3 minutes.

- Return scallops to soup and simmer 1 minute over low heat. Add chopped fresh parsley and cayenne pepper, and serve.

1 SERVING			
Calories	197	Carbohydrate	14 g
Protein	14 g	Fat	8 g
Fiber	1.8 g		

Fresh Clam Chowder

(4 servings)

36	fresh clams	36
3	potatoes, peeled and diced	3
2 tbsp	butter	30 mL
1	onion, diced	1
1	green pepper, diced	1
2 tbsp	all-purpose flour	30 mL
1½ cups	water	375 mL
1½ cups	clam juice	375 mL
2	green onions, chopped	2
1 cup	light cream, scalded	250 mL
1 tbsp	chopped fresh parsley	15 mL
	salt and pepper	
	few drops of Tabasco sauce	

- Steam fresh clams and reserve ½ cup (125 mL) steaming liquid. Chop clams and set aside.
- Pour reserved steaming liquid into a saucepan. Add potatoes and cover with water. Season and bring to a boil. Cook until potatoes are done. Drain and set aside.
- Heat butter in a saucepan over medium heat. Add onion and bell pepper; cook 2 minutes. Sprinkle in flour, mix well and cook 1 minute.
- Incorporate water and clam juice; mix well. Bring to a boil, season and cook 4 minutes over medium heat.
- Add potatoes, chopped clams, green onions and cream. Simmer soup 3 minutes.
- Add Tabasco sauce and correct seasoning. Sprinkle with parsley and serve.

1 SERVING

Calories	297	Carbohydrate	27 g
Protein	18 g	Fat	13 g
Fiber	2.3 g		

Beaufort Chowder

(4 to 6 servings)

2 oz	salt pork, diced	60 g
2	onions, finely chopped	2
1	garlic clove	1
2	large tomatoes, peeled, seeded and diced	2
3	potatoes, peeled and diced	3
5 cups	fish stock	1.25 L
½ tsp	thyme	2 mL
1 tsp	chopped fresh parsley	5 mL
2	red snapper fillets, cut in ½-inch (1 cm) wide strips	2
½ lb	shrimp, shelled and deveined	250 g
	pinch of crushed chilies	
	lime juice	
	salt and pepper	

- Place salt pork in a saucepan. Cook 4 minutes over medium heat. Remove salt pork and discard.
- Add onions and garlic to hot pan and cook 4 minutes over medium heat.
- Add tomatoes, mix well, and cook 2 minutes.
- Add potatoes, fish stock and seasonings. Bring to a boil and cook 10 minutes over medium heat. Do not cover.
- Add fish and shrimp, mix and cook 4 minutes over low heat. Add a few drops of lime juice. Serve with toasted garlic bread.

1 SERVING			
Calories	280	Carbohydrate	29 g
Protein	18 g	Fat	10 g
Fiber	1.2 g		

She-Crab Soup à la Mode

(4 to 6 servings)

2 tbsp	butter	30 mL
1	onion, grated	1
1	celery rib, grated	1
¼ tsp	mace	1 mL
2 tbsp	all-purpose flour	30 mL
2 cups	milk	500 mL
1½ cups	crabmeat, fresh or frozen, flaked	375 mL
½ cup	light cream	125 mL
2 tbsp	sherry	30 mL
	salt and pepper	

- Heat butter in a saucepan over medium heat. Add onion, celery and mace. Stir and cook 6 minutes over low heat.
- Sprinkle in flour and stir thoroughly. Cook 2 minutes. Season with salt and pepper.
- Incorporate milk using a whisk. Season again, and then bring to a boil. Cook 8 minutes over low heat, stirring occasionally.
- Add crabmeat and simmer 5 minutes.
- Incorporate cream and simmer 2 minutes.
- Add sherry, stir and simmer 1 minute. Serve.

1 SERVING			
Calories	201	Carbohydrate	11 g
Protein	12 g	Fat	12 g
Fiber	0 g		

Beaufort Bisque

(4 to 6 servings)

⅓ lb	fresh scallops, washed	150 g
⅓ lb	fresh shrimp, shelled and deveined	150 g
3 tbsp	butter	45 mL
1	small onion, finely chopped	1
½	celery rib, diced	½
3 tbsp	all-purpose flour	45 mL
3 cups	fish stock or light chicken stock, heated	750 mL
¼ tsp	ground fennel seed	1 mL
1 cup	milk or light cream, heated	250 mL
¼ cup	sherry	50 mL
1 tsp	chopped fresh parsley	5 mL
	lemon juice	
	paprika	
	salt and pepper	

- Place scallops and shrimp in a large sauté pan. Add lemon juice and pour in enough water to cover. Cover with a sheet of waxed paper, laid on the surface of the food, and bring to a boil.

- As soon as the water starts to boil, remove sauté pan from heat. Let seafood stand in hot liquid for 1 minute.

- Using a slotted spoon, remove seafood from liquid and set aside. Reserve cooking liquid.

- Heat butter in a saucepan over medium heat. Add onion and celery; cook 4 minutes over low heat.

- Sprinkle in flour, stir and cook 1 minute.

- Using a whisk, incorporate fish or chicken stock and reserved cooking liquid. Season with salt, pepper and fennel seed. Cook 8 minutes over low heat.

- Incorporate hot milk and simmer 3 minutes.

- Add seafood and simmer 2 minutes over low heat.

- Add sherry and simmer another 2 minutes.

- Sprinkle with parsley and paprika. Serve.

1 SERVING			
Calories	185	Carbohydrate	9 g
Protein	17 g	Fat	9 g
Fiber	0 g		

Appetizers

Tasty Shrimp Canapé Spread

(10 servings)

1½ lb	cooked shrimp, peeled and deveined	750 g
8	garlic cloves, blanched and peeled	8
2	shallots, chopped	2
2 tbsp	chopped fresh parsley	30 mL
¼ tsp	paprika	1 mL
1 tsp	Worcestershire sauce	5 mL
¼ lb	soft butter	125 g
	juice of 1 lemon	
	pinch of cayenne pepper	
	salt and pepper	

- Place all ingredients in a food processor. Blend 1 minute and correct seasoning.
- Transfer mixture to a bowl, cover and refrigerate 1 hour.
- Serve shrimp spread on toasted bread as an accompaniment to cocktails.

1 SERVING

Calories	185	Carbohydrate	3 g
Protein	19 g	Fat	11 g
Fiber	0 g		

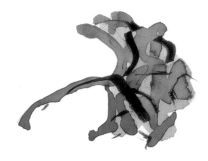

Deep-Fried Smelts

(4 servings)

1½ lb	fresh smelts, rinsed and dried	750 g
2 cups	all-purpose flour	500 mL
1 tsp	paprika	5 mL
3	eggs, beaten with a few drops of oil	3
2 cups	bread crumbs	500 mL
	salt and pepper	
	peanut oil for deep-frying	
	lemon wedges	

- Season smelts generously with salt and pepper. Dredge in flour seasoned with paprika. Dip smelts in beaten eggs and coat with bread crumbs.
- Preheat peanut oil to 350°F (180°C). Deep-fry smelts until golden brown. Drain on paper towels.
- Accompany with lemon wedges and serve.

1 SERVING			
Calories	764	Carbohydrate	64 g
Protein	91 g	Fat	16 g
Fiber	1.2 g		

Shrimp Egg Rolls

(4 servings)

2 tbsp	olive oil	30 mL
½ lb	fresh mushrooms, cleaned and julienned	250 g
8	green onions, cut in ¾-inch (2 cm) lengths	8
1	celery rib, julienned	1
3	garlic cloves, smashed and chopped	3
1	Chinese cabbage leaf, thinly sliced	1
1½ cups	bean sprouts	375 mL
1 tbsp	soy sauce	15 mL
12	shrimp, cooked, peeled, deveined and thinly sliced	12
1 tbsp	cornstarch	15 mL
2 tbsp	cold water	30 mL
	salt and pepper	
	few drops of Tabasco sauce	
	egg roll wrappers	
	peanut oil for deep-frying	

- Heat olive oil in a frying pan over medium heat. Add mushrooms, green onions, celery, garlic and cabbage. Cook 3 minutes over high heat.

- Add bean sprouts and soy sauce. Season well, cover and cook 3 to 4 minutes over low heat. Add a few drops of Tabasco sauce.

- Stir in shrimp and season well. If mixture is too dry, add a little water.

- Dilute cornstarch in cold water, incorporate into mixture and cook 1 minute over low heat.

- Remove pan from heat and let cool. Preheat peanut oil to 375°F (190°C).

- Place a small amount of shrimp stuffing in the middle of an egg roll wrapper. Fold one side over stuffing and cover with opposite side. Wet ends with a little water to seal; press together gently. Repeat with remaining stuffing and wrappers. Deep-fry in peanut oil until golden brown.

- Drain on paper towels and serve.

1 SERVING			
Calories	174	Carbohydrate	14 g
Protein	7 g	Fat	10 g
Fiber	2.1 g		

Stuffed Fresh Clams

(4 servings)

32	fresh clams, cleaned	32
1 cup	water	250 mL
3 tbsp	butter	45 mL
2	onions, chopped	2
2 tbsp	chopped fresh parsley	30 mL
4	garlic cloves, smashed and chopped	4
¾ lb	fresh mushrooms, cleaned and chopped	375 g
1 cup	coarse white bread crumbs	250 mL
½ cup	heavy cream	125 mL
	salt and pepper	
	few drops of Tabasco sauce	

- Place clams and water in a saucepan. Cover and cook over medium heat until shells open.

- Remove clams from pan and detach from shells. Chop clams and set aside. Twist apart shells and dry well; arrange in a single layer in a roasting pan. Strain cooking liquid through a sieve lined with cheesecloth and reserve.

- Heat butter in a frying pan over medium heat. Add onions and cook 4 minutes. Add parsley, garlic and mushrooms; season well. Cook 5 minutes over high heat.

- Add chopped clams and bread crumbs. Mix well and incorporate some of the strained cooking liquid. Add cream and Tabasco sauce; season well. Mixture should not be too thin.

- Fill shells with stuffing and broil 8 minutes or until lightly browned. Serve.

1 SERVING			
Calories	454	Carbohydrate	33 g
Protein	31 g	Fat	22 g
Fiber	3.4 g		

Oysters au Gratin on the Half Shell

(4 servings)

32	fresh oysters, shucked, reserving bottom shells	32
½ cup	dry white wine	125 mL
2 tbsp	olive oil	30 mL
2	onions, peeled and chopped	2
3	garlic cloves, smashed and chopped	3
½ lb	fresh mushrooms, cleaned and finely chopped	250 g
2 tbsp	chopped fresh basil	30 mL
2 tbsp	chopped fresh parsley	30 mL
1 cup	coarse white bread crumbs	250 mL
¼ cup	heavy cream	50 mL
	salt and pepper	

- Place oysters and wine in a frying pan; season well. Cover with a sheet of waxed paper, laid on the surface of the food, and bring to a boil. Remove from heat immediately, cool slightly and chop oysters.

- Heat oil in another frying pan over medium heat. Add onions and garlic; cook 3 minutes.

- Add mushrooms and all seasonings; cook 6 minutes over high heat. Stir in chopped oysters and bread crumbs. Pour in cream, stir well and cook 1 minute over medium heat.

- Fill shells with stuffing and broil 3 minutes or until lightly browned. Serve.

1 SERVING			
Calories	339	Carbohydrate	34 g
Protein	12 g	Fat	15 g
Fiber	3 g		

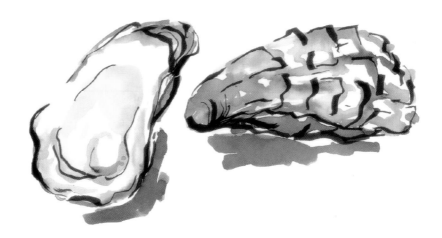

Mussels au Gratin

(4 servings)

9 lb	mussels (or clams), scrubbed and washed	4.5 kg
½ cup	dry white wine	125 mL
3	slices white bread, crusts removed	3
½ cup	milk	125 mL
2 tbsp	butter	30 mL
½ cup	chopped shallots	125 mL
4	garlic cloves, smashed and chopped	4
4 tbsp	chopped fresh parsley	60 mL
2 tbsp	chopped fresh chives	30 mL
	pinch cayenne pepper	
	salt and pepper	

- Place mussels in a very large saucepan. Add wine, cover and cook over medium heat just until shells open. Shake pan 2 or 3 times during cooking. Discard any mussels that do not open.

- Remove mussels from shells, drain well and chop. Set aside. Pour liquid from shells back into pan. Set shells aside.

- Line a sieve with cheesecloth and strain cooking liquid into a small saucepan. Place pan on stove and cook 5 minutes over high heat. Set aside.

- Place bread in a bowl and cover with milk; set aside to soak.

- Heat butter in a frying pan over medium heat. Add shallots and garlic; cook 4 minutes.

- Add parsley, chives and cayenne pepper. Cook 1 minute.

- Add chopped mussels and season well. Stir and then remove pan from heat.

- Squeeze out excess milk from bread and incorporate bread into mussel mixture. Add reduced cooking liquid and stir together well.

- Fill shells with stuffing and broil in oven for 3 minutes. Serve.

1 SERVING			
Calories	560	Carbohydrate	39 g
Protein	76 g	Fat	9 g
Fiber	1 g		

Shrimp Cocktail

(4 servings)

¾ cup	mayonnaise	175 mL
2 tbsp	chili sauce	30 mL
1 tsp	Worcestershire sauce	5 mL
1 tbsp	whisky	15 mL
24	large shrimp, cooked, peeled and deveined	24
	salt and pepper	
	lemon juice to taste	
	lemon wedges	

- Mix mayonnaise with remaining ingredients, except shrimp and lemon wedges. Correct seasoning.
- Serve shrimp with the cocktail sauce and lemon wedges.

1 SERVING

Calories	360	Carbohydrate	3 g
Protein	7 g	Fat	32 g
Fiber	0.5 g		

Savannah Steamed Shrimp

(4 servings)

1¼ lb	large shrimp, washed	625 g
1 tsp	black pepper	5 mL
½ tsp	paprika	2 mL
	pinch of crushed chilies	
	salt	

- Mix ingredients together in a bowl and refrigerate 2 hours.
- Steam shrimp 6 to 7 minutes, stirring 2 to 3 times during cooking.
- Serve with fresh lemon wedges.

1 SERVING			
Calories	194	Carbohydrate	5 g
Protein	39 g	Fat	2 g
Fiber	1 g		

Cold Shrimp with Curry Dressing and Fruit

(4 servings)

1½ lb	fresh shrimp	750 g
1 tbsp	olive oil	15 mL
1	onion, chopped	1
2	shallots, chopped	2
2	garlic cloves, smashed and chopped	2
1 tbsp	curry powder	15 mL
½ cup	mayonnaise	125 mL
2 tbsp	chili sauce	30 mL
2 tbsp	sour cream	30 mL
1 cup	canned mandarin segments, drained	250 mL
2	apples, cored, peeled and sliced	2
	salt and pepper	
	few drops of Tabasco sauce	

- Place shrimp in a saucepan filled with cold, salted water. Place over medium heat and bring to a boil. Remove pan from heat and let stand 2 minutes.

- Place pan under cold, running water to stop cooking process. Peel and devein shrimp.

- Heat oil in a frying pan over medium heat. Add onion, shallots and garlic; cook 4 minutes over low heat. Season well.

- Sprinkle in curry powder and mix well. Cook 3 minutes.

- Transfer vegetable mixture to bowl. Incorporate mayonnaise, chili sauce and sour cream. Add a few drops of Tabasco sauce. Mix well and season to taste.

- Add fruit and combine gently.

- Arrange shrimp on serving plates and top with dressing. Accompany with nuts, grapes and greens if desired.

1 SERVING			
Calories	521	Carbohydrate	28 g
Protein	37 g	Fat	29 g
Fiber	2.5 g		

Tomatoes Stuffed with Shrimp Remoulade

(6 to 8 servings)

8	small tomatoes, hollowed out	8
¾ lb	cooked shrimp, peeled, deveined and chopped	375 g
½	celery rib, finely chopped	½
2	green onions, finely chopped	2
2 tbsp	chopped pimento	30 mL
1 tsp	horseradish	5 mL
1 tbsp	Dijon mustard	15 mL
2 tbsp	chopped fresh parsley	30 mL
3 tbsp	wine vinegar	45 mL
¼ cup	olive oil	50 mL
	juice of ½ lemon	
	salt, pepper, paprika	

- Season each tomato cavity with salt and pepper; set aside.
- Place shrimp, celery, green onions and pimento in a bowl. Season with salt and pepper. Set aside.
- Mix horseradish, mustard and parsley together in another bowl. Season with salt, pepper and paprika. Whisk in vinegar. Add oil in a thin stream, whisking constantly.
- Pour dressing over shrimp mixture and mix well. Stir in lemon juice, and stuff tomatoes with mixture. Serve.

1 SERVING			
Calories	156	Carbohydrate	7 g
Protein	14 g	Fat	8 g
Fiber	1 g		

Tropical Scampi

(4 servings)

24	large scampi	24
½ cup	mayonnaise	125 mL
1 tsp	curry powder	5 mL
1 tbsp	chopped fresh parsley	15 mL
⅓ cup	mango chutney	75 mL
1 tsp	Dijon mustard	5 mL
1 tbsp	chopped fresh fennel leaves	15 mL
¼ cup	toasted slivered almonds	50 mL
	juice of 1 lemon	
	salt and pepper	
	lettuce leaves for garnishing	

- Place scampi in a saucepan and cover with water. Add some lemon juice, season and bring to a boil. Remove immediately from heat and let stand 3 minutes.

- Place pan under cold running water to stop the cooking process. Using scissors, peel scampi and devein. Rinse under cold water and pat dry with paper towels.

- Place whole scampi in a bowl and season well. Add lemon juice to taste.

- In another bowl, mix mayonnaise with curry powder, parsley, chutney, Dijon mustard and fennel. Season and mix well.

- Line scallop shells or small dishes with lettuce leaves, and top with scampi. Sprinkle with lemon juice and almonds. Serve with curry dressing.

1 SERVING			
Calories	417	Carbohydrate	11 g
Protein	28 g	Fat	29 g
Fiber	0.8 g		

Cold Lobster and Shrimp

(4 servings)

4	1½ lb (750 g) live lobsters	4
½ cup	mayonnaise	125 mL
2 tbsp	capers	30 mL
2 tbsp	chili sauce	30 mL
4	hard-boiled eggs, halved	4
⅓ lb	shrimp, cooked, peeled and deveined	150 g
	salt and pepper	
	few drops of Tabasco sauce	
	lemon juice to taste	

- Fill a large pot with salted water. Bring to a boil over high heat. Plunge live lobsters into water. Cover until water resumes boil and cook 15 minutes over medium heat. Shells will turn bright red when cooked.

- Remove lobsters from water and let cool on counter.

- Cut lobsters in half. Discard intestinal sac. Remove meat from body and claws. Slice and set aside. Clean shells and dry in a warm oven.

- Mix mayonnaise with capers, chili sauce, salt, pepper and Tabasco sauce. Force hard-boiled egg yolks through a wire sieve; incorporate into mixture. Season well and add lemon juice.

- Serve lobster meat in lobster shells with mayonnaise mixture. Place two hard-boiled egg white halves on each serving and fill with shrimp. Top with more mayonnaise sauce. Garnish with lemon wedges and serve.

1 SERVING

Calories	763	Carbohydrate	9 g
Protein	112 g	Fat	31 g
Fiber	0 g		

Maryland Crab Cakes

(6 servings)

2	slices white bread, crusts removed	2
¼ cup	milk	50 mL
1 lb	crabmeat, fresh or frozen and thawed, flaked	500 g
3	green onions, chopped	3
¼ cup	mayonnaise	50 mL
1 tsp	Worcestershire sauce	5 mL
1 tsp	dry mustard	5 mL
¼ tsp	cayenne pepper	1 mL
	juice of ½ lemon	
	salt	
	peanut oil	

- Place bread in a bowl and cover with milk. Soak 5 minutes.
- Squeeze out excess milk from bread and place in a clean bowl. Add remaining ingredients to bread and mix well. Cover and refrigerate 2 hours.
- Shape mixture into thick patties. Cook in hot peanut oil over medium heat, about 4 to 5 minutes or until nicely browned.
- Serve with fresh lemon.

1 SERVING			
Calories	235	Carbohydrate	14 g
Protein	24 g	Fat	9 g
Fiber	1 g		

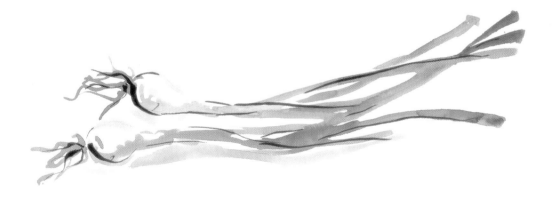

Tuna Spinach Pâté

(6 servings)

2	cans solid Albacore tuna, drained	2
1 tbsp	chopped fresh parsley	15 mL
1½ cups	cooked spinach, chopped	375 mL
2 tbsp	capers	30 mL
⅓ cup	whipped cream	75 mL
2 tbsp	sour cream	30 mL
	salt and pepper	
	Tabasco sauce	

- Place tuna, parsley, spinach and capers in food processor and purée. Season generously, add Tabasco sauce to taste and blend to incorporate.

- Transfer mixture to a bowl and fold in whipped cream and sour cream. Fill buttered custard or terrine mold with mixture. Cover with plastic wrap, ensuring that wrap touches surface. Refrigerate 8 hours.

- Remove from mold and place on serving platter, if desired. Accompany with chutney, assorted crackers and crudités.

1 SERVING

Calories	114	Carbohydrate	2 g
Protein	13 g	Fat	6 g
Fiber	1.2 g		

Smoked Salmon on Potato Pancakes

(4 servings)

4	large potatoes	4
1	onion, grated	1
3 tbsp	all-purpose flour	45 mL
1	large egg, separated	1
2 tbsp	olive oil	30 mL
16	thin slices smoked salmon	16
	sour cream	
	salt and pepper	

• Peel and grate potatoes. Place grated potatoes in a large bowl and cover with cold water. Let stand 15 minutes, then drain well. Squeeze out excess liquid from potatoes.

• Place potatoes in the bowl of an electric mixer. Add onion and flour, and season. Mix well. Add egg yolk and mix again.

• Beat egg white lightly and incorporate into mixture.

• Shape mixture into small patties. Refrigerate 1 hour.

• Heat half of the olive oil in a frying pan over medium heat. Add half of the potato pancakes and cook 5 minutes on each side. Season well. Remove pancakes from pan and keep hot in oven. Add remaining oil and repeat procedure for remaining pancakes.

• Roll up slices of salmon and serve on potato pancakes. Accompany with sour cream.

1 SERVING			
Calories	296	Carbohydrate	35 g
Protein	10 g	Fat	13 g
Fiber	3 g		

Salads

Salade Niçoise

(4 to 6 servings)

8	anchovy fillets	8
2 lb	tomatoes, cored and quartered	1 kg
1	cucumber, peeled, seeded and sliced	1
½ lb	green beans, pared and blanched	250 g
1	green pepper, sliced	1
1	yellow pepper, sliced	1
1 cup	pitted green olives	250 mL
1 tbsp	chopped fresh parsley	15 mL
4	blanched garlic cloves, puréed	4
6–8 tbsp	olive oil	90–120 mL
2 tbsp	chopped fresh basil	30 mL
3	hard-boiled eggs, quartered	3
	cleaned mixed greens for presentation	
	salt and pepper	
	juice of 1½ lemons	

- Soak anchovy fillets in cold water. Drain well and pat dry with paper towels. Coarsely chop.

- Line serving platter with mixed greens. Set aside.

- Place vegetables, olives, anchovies and parsley in a bowl. Season generously and mix well.

- In another bowl, mix garlic with lemon juice, salt and pepper. Whisk in oil and basil. Pour dressing over salad ingredients and mix well.

- Spoon salad onto serving platter. Stud with wedges of hard-boiled egg and season with pepper.

1 SERVING			
Calories	291	Carbohydrate	14 g
Protein	7 g	Fat	23 g
Fiber	3.3 g		

Salmon Salad

(4 servings)

2 cups	flaked cooked salmon	500 mL
2	hard-boiled eggs, diced	2
½	cucumber, peeled, seeded and diced	½
1	red pepper, diced (optional)	1
⅓ cup	light mayonnaise	75 mL
	salt, pepper, paprika	

- Place salmon in a bowl. Add eggs and mix gently.
- Add remaining ingredients and mix.
- Serve on lettuce leaves.

1 SERVING			
Calories	268	Carbohydrate	5 g
Protein	23 g	Fat	17 g
Fiber	0 g		

Cold Halibut with Assorted Vegetables

(2 servings)

1	cooked halibut steak, flaked	1
½	large tomato, cored and quartered	½
1 cup	cooked cauliflower florets	250 mL
2 tbsp	chopped fresh parsley	30 mL
6	stuffed green olives, sliced	6
8	cooked baby carrots	8
2 tbsp	wine vinegar	30 mL
1	garlic clove, smashed and chopped	1
3 tbsp	olive oil	45 mL
	salt and pepper	
	hard-boiled egg slices	

- Place fish in a bowl with tomato, cauliflower, half the parsley, olives and carrots; season well.

- Place vinegar, garlic, remaining parsley, salt and pepper in separate bowl. Whisk together. Incorporate oil gradually while whisking constantly.

- Pour vinaigrette over salad ingredients and toss gently. Serve with slices of hard-boiled egg and lettuce leaves, if desired.

1 SERVING			
Calories	450	Carbohydrate	26 g
Protein	22 g	Fat	29 g
Fiber	8 g		

69

Potato and Tuna Salad

(4 servings)

1	6.5-oz (184 g) can tuna, drained	1
3	large cooked potatoes, still hot, cubed	3
4 tbsp	cooked chopped red onion	60 mL
2	green onions, chopped	2
1	bell pepper, cubed	1
1	celery rib, diced	1
2 tbsp	wine vinegar	30 mL
2 tbsp	lemon juice	30 mL
1½ tbsp	Dijon mustard	22 mL
¼ cup	heavy cream	50 mL
	salt and pepper	

- Place tuna in a large bowl. Add vegetables and mix.
- Pour vinegar and lemon juice in another bowl. Add mustard, salt and pepper; whisk together.
- Whisk in cream. Pour dressing over salad and toss well. Marinate 15 minutes before serving.

1 SERVING

Calories	238	Carbohydrate	30 g
Protein	16 g	Fat	6 g
Fiber	3.2 g		

Salmon Trout Salad with Walnut Oil Vinaigrette

(4 servings)

½ cup	dry white wine	125 mL
1 cup	water	250 mL
4	salmon trout fillets, unskinned	4
1 tbsp	balsamic vinegar	15 mL
1 tbsp	walnut oil	15 mL
2 tbsp	peanut oil	30 mL
1 tbsp	chopped fresh chervil	15 mL
½ lb	mesclun (mixed baby greens)	250 g
1	lemon, peeled and sliced	1
	juice of ½ lemon	
	salt and pepper	

• Place wine, water and lemon juice in a large sauté pan. Bring to a boil and cook 4 minutes over medium heat. Reduce heat to low and add fish fillets; cook 4 minutes.

• Meanwhile, prepare the vinaigrette: combine balsamic vinegar, walnut oil, peanut oil and chervil; season to taste.

• Drain fish and cut each fillet in half; place two pieces on each plate. Serve with mesclun. Drizzle vinaigrette over salad and garnish with lemon slices.

●

Note: Mesclun, originally from the south of France, is a mixture of different salad greens and young shoots such as lamb's lettuce, endive, radicchio and rocket lettuce. The name is derived from the Niçois word "mesclumo", meaning *mixture*.

1 SERVING			
Calories	205	Carbohydrate	3 g
Protein	19 g	Fat	13 g
Fiber	0.9 g		

Shrimp and Artichoke Bottoms

(4 servings)

DRESSING		
½ cup	mayonnaise	125 mL
2 tbsp	ketchup	30 mL
2 tbsp	chili sauce	30 mL
1 tsp	horseradish	5 mL
2 tbsp	sour cream	30 mL
	salt and pepper	
	few drops of Tabasco sauce	

SALAD		
1 lb	fresh shrimp	500 g
4	artichoke bottoms, cooked and sliced	4
1	red onion, sliced in rings	1
1	apple, cored, peeled and sliced	1
1	celery rib, thinly sliced	1
	salt, pepper and lemon juice	
	lettuce	
	lemon slices	

- Mix all dressing ingredients together in a small bowl. Correct seasoning and set aside.

- Place shrimp in a saucepan and cover with cold water. Add salt and lemon juice; bring to a boil. As soon as the water boils, remove pan from the heat. Stir shrimp and let stand 2 minutes. Place pan under cold running water until shrimp cool. Remove from water, peel and devein.

- Place shrimp in a large bowl. Add artichoke bottoms, onion, apple and celery. Season with salt and pepper. Pour in vinaigrette and mix well. Sprinkle with more lemon juice.

- Line serving plates with lettuce. Top with shrimp salad and garnish with lemon slices. Serve.

1 SERVING			
Calories	404	Carbohydrate	20 g
Protein	27 g	Fat	24 g
Fiber	1.9 g		

Shrimp Remoulade

(4 to 6 servings)

1	small celeriac, peeled and julienned	1
4 tbsp	mayonnaise	60 mL
1 tsp	Dijon mustard	5 mL
2 tbsp	sour cream	30 mL
1 lb	cooked shrimp, peeled, deveined and cut in two	500 g
2 tbsp	finely chopped lemon rind	30 mL
1	small green pepper, julienned	1
	lemon juice	
	salt, pepper, paprika	

- Cook celeriac 3 minutes in boiling, salted water with lemon juice. Place saucepan under cold running water to stop the cooking process, and then drain celeriac well. Squeeze out excess liquid from celeriac and blot with paper towels.

- Place mayonnaise in a bowl. Add mustard and sour cream. Mix and add salt, pepper, paprika and lemon juice to taste. Mix again.

- Place celeriac, shrimp, lemon rind and green pepper in another bowl. Add sauce and mix well. Correct seasoning and serve.

1 SERVING			
Calories	194	Carbohydrate	6 g
Protein	25 g	Fat	8 g
Fiber	1.3 g		

Fresh Mussels in Salad

(4 servings)

3 lb	fresh mussels, washed, bearded and scrubbed	1.5 kg
1	head Boston lettuce	1
1 tbsp	olive oil	15 mL
2	shallots, chopped	2
1	garlic clove, smashed and chopped	1
1	celery rib, sliced	1
12	cherry tomatoes, halved	12
1 tbsp	chopped fresh basil	15 mL
1 cup	heavy cream	250 mL
2 tbsp	buttermilk	30 mL
3 tbsp	fresh lime juice	45 mL
	salt and pepper	

- Place mussels in a large saucepan; cover and bring to a boil. Cook over low heat until shells open, about 5 minutes. Shake pan several times during cooking to mix mussels.

- Remove mussels from pan, discarding the shells and any unopened mussels. Strain cooking liquid through a sieve lined with cheesecloth, reserving ¼ cup (50 mL) liquid.

- Tear lettuce leaves into smaller pieces. Place in a large bowl with mussels. Set aside.

- Heat oil in a frying pan over medium heat. Add shallots, garlic, celery, tomatoes and basil. Season well and cook 2 minutes. Pour over salad and toss gently.

- Mix reserved cooking liquid with heavy cream in a small bowl. Add buttermilk and lime juice. Mix well and season to taste. Pour mixture over salad, toss and serve.

1 SERVING			
Calories	557	Carbohydrate	21 g
Protein	44 g	Fat	33 g
Fiber	1.3 g		

Seafood Salad with Roasted Peppers

(4 servings)

DRESSING

1 tbsp	Dijon mustard	15 mL
1	egg yolk	1
1 tbsp	chopped fresh chives	15 mL
1 tsp	chopped fresh parsley	5 mL
2	blanched garlic cloves, puréed	2
3 tbsp	white wine vinegar	45 mL
½ cup	olive oil	125 mL
2 tbsp	sour cream	30 mL
	salt and pepper	

SALAD

1	green pepper	1
1	yellow pepper	1
3	halibut steaks, cooked	3
12	shrimp, cooked, peeled and deveined	12
1	large apple, cored, peeled and sliced	1
2	celery ribs, thinly sliced	2
	salt and pepper	
	lemon juice to taste	

- In a bowl, whisk together mustard, egg yolk, chives, parsley and garlic.

- Add vinegar and season well; whisk again. Add oil and whisk to incorporate. Mix in sour cream and set aside.

- Cut peppers in half and remove seeds. Oil skins and place cut-side-down on a cookie sheet; broil 6 minutes. Remove from oven and let cool in a large bowl covered with plastic wrap. Peel off skin, slice peppers and return to bowl.

- Remove skin and bones from halibut. Flake fish and add to bowl.

- Cut shrimp in half. Add to bowl along with remaining salad ingredients.

- Pour in vinaigrette and toss well. Season generously with salt and pepper. Serve on a bed of lettuce if desired.

1 SERVING			
Calories	447	Carbohydrate	10 g
Protein	23 g	Fat	35 g
Fiber	1.5 g		

Mayonnaise

(makes about 1½ cups/375 mL)

2	egg yolks	2
1 tsp	Dijon mustard	5 mL
1¼ cups	olive oil	300 mL
	juice of 1 lemon	
	salt and pepper	

- Place egg yolks in a bowl. Add mustard and mix well. Season with salt and pepper.
- Add oil, drop by drop, whisking constantly. When mayonnaise begins to thicken, add oil in a steady stream, whisking constantly.
- Add lemon juice only after mayonnaise is very thick.

●

Note: To store mayonnaise for 2 days in the refrigerator, add 1 tbsp (15 mL) hot water. Whisk well and store covered.

1 RECIPE

Calories	2076	Carbohydrate	4 g
Protein	4 g	Fat	228 g
Fiber	0 g		

Mousseline Mayonnaise

(makes about 1¾ cups/425 mL)

2	egg yolks	2
1 tbsp	Dijon mustard	15 mL
1 tsp	wine vinegar	5 mL
1 tbsp	curry powder	15 mL
1 tsp	chopped shallot	5 mL
1 tsp	chopped fresh parsley	5 mL
1¼ cups	olive oil	300 mL
¼ cup	whipped cream	50 mL
	salt and pepper	

- Place egg yolks in a bowl. Add mustard, vinegar, curry powder, shallot and parsley. Whisk together.
- Add oil in a thin stream, whisking constantly. Season with salt and pepper.
- Fold in whipped cream. Serve mayonnaise with vegetables, fish or salads.

1 RECIPE

Calories	2632	Carbohydrate	0 g
Protein	4 g	Fat	292 g
Fiber	0 g		

Homemade Herb Mayonnaise

(makes about 1½ cups/375 mL)

2	egg yolks	2
1 tbsp	Dijon mustard	15 mL
1¼ cups	olive oil	300 mL
2 tsp	wine vinegar	10 mL
1 tsp	chopped fresh parsley	5 mL
1 tsp	chopped fresh tarragon	5 mL
1 tsp	chopped fresh chives	5 mL
	lemon juice	
	salt and pepper	

• Place egg yolks and mustard in a bowl; whisk together.

• Add oil in a thin stream, whisking constantly. Increase flow as mixture thickens. When mixture is very thick and before all the oil is incorporated, whisk in vinegar and lemon juice.

• Incorporate remaining oil, adding more if necessary.

• Stir in fresh herbs and season generously. Use immediately in a variety of fresh salads.

●

Note: To store mayonnaise for 2 days in the refrigerator, add 1 tbsp (15 mL) hot water. Whisk well and store covered.

1 RECIPE			
Calories	2791	Carbohydrate	1 g
Protein	6 g	Fat	307 g

Garlic Vinaigrette

(makes about 1 cup/250 mL)

4	garlic cloves	4
1 tbsp	Dijon mustard	15 mL
2	shallots, chopped	2
¼ cup	wine vinegar or balsamic vinegar	50 mL
¾ cup	olive oil	175 mL
	salt and pepper	
	lemon juice	

• Blanch garlic cloves in salted, boiling water for 4 minutes. Peel and purée.

• Place all ingredients, except lemon juice, in a bowl. Whisk together until thick.

• Add lemon juice and correct seasoning. Whisk again before using.

1 RECIPE			
Calories	1706	Carbohydrate	7 g
Protein	1 g	Fat	186 g

Lemon Vinaigrette

(makes about 1 cup/250 mL)

1 tbsp	Dijon mustard	15 mL
6 tbsp	lemon juice	90 mL
½ cup	olive oil	125 mL
2 tbsp	sour cream	30 mL
	salt and pepper	
	few drops of Tabasco sauce	

• Place all ingredients except sour cream in a bowl. Whisk together until well-incorporated.

• Add sour cream and correct seasoning. Whisk again before using.

1 RECIPE			
Calories	1196	Carbohydrate	9 g
Protein	2 g	Fat	128 g

Basic Vinaigrette

(makes about 1 cup/250 mL)

1 tbsp	Dijon mustard	15 mL
2	shallots, chopped	2
1 tbsp	chopped fresh parsley	15 mL
¼ cup	wine vinegar or balsamic vinegar	50 mL
¾ cup	olive oil	175 mL
	salt and pepper	
	lemon or lime juice	

- Place all ingredients, except lemon juice, in a bowl. Whisk together until thick.
- Add lemon juice to taste and correct seasoning. Whisk again before using.

1 RECIPE

Calories	1485	Carbohydrate	8 g
Protein	1 g	Fat	161 g

Yogurt Dressing

(makes about ¾ cup/175 mL)

½ cup	plain yogurt	125 mL
1 tsp	honey	5 mL
¼ cup	lemon juice	50 mL
1 tsp	chopped fresh chives	5 mL
	salt and pepper	

- Place all ingredients in a bowl. Whisk together until well incorporated. Correct seasoning. Whisk again before using.

1 SERVING

Calories	122	Carbohydrate	19 g
Protein	7 g	Fat	2 g

Garlic Croutons

(makes about 6 cups/1.5 L)

1	loaf stale French bread	1
¼ cup	olive oil	50 mL
4	large garlic cloves, smashed and chopped	4

- Trim crusts off bread. Cut into wide slices and dice. Toast pieces on all sides in oven, under the broiler.
- Heat oil in a large frying pan over high heat. Add toasted bread and garlic. Cook 3 minutes, stirring frequently.
- Drain croutons on paper towels. Cool before using and store in an airtight container to preserve crispness.

1 RECIPE

Calories	1128	Carbohydrate	142 g
Protein	23 g	Fat	52 g
Fiber	4 g		

Pasta and Rice

Poached Scallops with Capers

(4 servings)

1½ lb	fresh scallops, washed	750 g
1½ cups	water	375 mL
1	celery rib, diced	1
1	carrot, sliced	1
¼ tsp	fennel seed	1 mL
1	fresh tarragon sprig	1
½ cup	dry white wine	125 mL
3 tbsp	butter, softened	45 mL
1½ tbsp	all-purpose flour	22 mL
1½ tbsp	fresh chopped dill	22 mL
2 tbsp	capers	30 mL
	lemon juice	
	pinch of cayenne pepper	
	salt and pepper	

- Place scallops, water, celery, carrot, lemon juice, fennel seed, tarragon, cayenne and black pepper in a sauté pan.
- Pour in wine and cover with a sheet of waxed paper, laid on the surface of the food. Bring to a boil over medium heat. As soon as the liquid starts to boil, remove pan from heat. Let stand 2 minutes.
- Remove scallops using a slotted spoon. Set aside in a bowl.
- Return sauté pan to stove over high heat. Bring to a boil and cook 3 minutes. Season well, and then pour sauce through a sieve into a bowl.
- Pour half of the strained liquid back into the sauté pan over low heat. Mix butter with flour. Incorporate into cooking liquid, whisking constantly until sauce thickens.
- Add dill and capers. Place scallops in sauce and warm a few minutes over low heat.
- Serve over noodles.

1 SERVING			
Calories	370	Carbohydrate	11 g
Protein	44 g	Fat	15 g
Fiber	1 g		

Agnolotti with Anchovy Pesto

(4 servings)

5	garlic cloves, peeled	5
¾ cup	pine nuts	175 mL
6 to 8	anchovy fillets, drained	6 to 8
1 cup	fresh basil	250 mL
¼ cup	olive oil	50 mL
½ cup	grated Parmesan cheese	125 mL
4	portions cooked agnolotti pasta, hot	4
	pepper	

- Place garlic, pine nuts, anchovies and basil in food processor. Blend for 30 seconds.
- Add oil and cheese; blend to incorporate.
- Pour sauce over hot pasta and season with pepper. Mix and serve.

1 SERVING

Calories	382	Carbohydrate	38 g
Protein	13 g	Fat	20 g
Fiber	1.4 g		

Rigatoni with Shrimp

(4 servings)

1 tbsp	olive oil	15 mL
¾ lb	shrimp, shelled, deveined, washed and halved	375 g
3	shallots, chopped	3
½ lb	fresh mushrooms, cleaned and halved	250 g
1 tbsp	chopped fresh ginger	15 mL
3	tomatoes, peeled and chopped	3
1 tbsp	chopped fresh basil	15 mL
4	portions cooked rigatoni, hot	4
	salt and pepper	
	pinch of crushed chilies	

- Heat oil in a frying pan over medium heat. Add shrimp and cook 2 minutes over high heat. Turn shrimp over and continue cooking 1 minute. Remove shrimp from pan and set aside.
- Add shallots, mushrooms and ginger to pan. Season and cook 5 minutes over high heat.
- Add tomatoes, basil and crushed chilies. Season and cook 8 minutes over medium heat.
- Return shrimp to pan and simmer 3 minutes over low heat.
- Add hot pasta, mix and simmer another 3 minutes. Serve.

1 SERVING			
Calories	357	Carbohydrate	48 g
Protein	31 g	Fat	5 g
Fiber	3 g		

Seafood Linguine with Fresh Vegetables
(4 servings)

32	fresh clams, scrubbed and washed	32
1 cup	water	250 mL
1 tbsp	olive oil	15 mL
3	shallots, chopped	3
2	garlic cloves, smashed and chopped	2
2	green onions, chopped	2
1	red pepper, diced	1
2	large tomatoes, peeled and chopped	2
1 tbsp	chopped fresh tarragon	15 mL
4	portions cooked linguine, hot	4
	juice of 1 lemon	
	salt and pepper	

- Place clams in a saucepan. Pour in water and add lemon juice. Cover and cook 5 minutes, stirring once during cooking. Remove saucepan from heat. All clam shells should be fully opened. Discard unopened clams. Let clams stand in cooking liquid to keep warm.

- Heat oil in a sauté pan over medium heat. Add shallots, garlic and green onions. Mix and cook 4 minutes over low heat.

- Add red pepper and tomatoes. Season, add tarragon and cook 12 minutes over medium heat.

- Place linguine on plates. Arrange clams, still in their shells, on pasta. Ladle sauce over the top and serve.

Note: Choose firm shallots with dry skins. Wrap peeled bulbs in plastic and keep in the refrigerator. They lose their flavor after 24 hours.

1 SERVING

Calories	308	Carbohydrate	47 g
Protein	17 g	Fat	6 g
Fiber	1.5 g		

Fettuccine with Fresh Mussels

(4 servings)

2 lb	fresh mussels, scrubbed and washed	1 kg
¼ cup	water	50 mL
1 tbsp	olive oil	15 mL
2	garlic cloves, smashed and chopped	2
¼ cup	dry white wine	50 mL
2 tbsp	beurre manié (see page 160)	30 mL
1 tbsp	chopped fresh parsley	15 mL
4	portions cooked fettuccine, hot	4
	juice of 1 lemon	
	salt and pepper	

• Place mussels in a large saucepan. Add lemon juice, water and pepper. Cover and cook over medium heat until shells open.

• Remove saucepan from heat. Discard unopened mussels. Remove mussels from shells, place in a bowl and set aside. Pour any juices left in shells back into saucepan.

• Strain cooking liquid from mussels through a sieve lined with cheesecloth. Set aside.

• Heat oil in a frying pan over medium heat. Add garlic and cook 2 minutes.

• Pour in wine and cook 2 minutes over high heat.

• Stir in cooking liquid from mussels and season well. Cook 2 minutes, then remove pan from heat.

• Incorporate beurre manié using a whisk. Sprinkle with chopped parsley and season with pepper. Add hot pasta and mussels to sauce, stir and serve.

1 SERVING			
Calories	358	Carbohydrate	39 g
Protein	21 g	Fat	12 g
Fiber	0 g		

Fresh Scallops in White Wine over Pasta

(4 servings)

2	shallots, chopped	2
½ lb	fresh mushrooms, cleaned and cut in three	250 g
1 lb	fresh scallops	500 g
1 tbsp	chopped fresh parsley	15 mL
½ cup	dry white wine	125 mL
1½ cups	clam juice	375 mL
2 tbsp	butter	30 mL
2 tbsp	flour	30 mL
½ cup	grated Gruyère cheese	125 mL
4	portions cooked rotini (spiral pasta), hot	4
	salt and pepper	
	grated Parmesan cheese	

- Place shallots, mushrooms, scallops, parsley, wine and clam juice in a sauté pan. Season with salt and pepper. Cover with a sheet of waxed paper, touching the surface of the food. Bring to a boil over medium heat, then remove immediately from heat. Let stand 3 minutes.

- Use a slotted spoon to remove scallops. Transfer to a bowl and set aside.

- Return sauté pan to stove. Cook contents of pan 7 minutes over medium heat. Set aside.

- Heat butter in a saucepan over medium heat. Add flour, stir with a wooden spoon and cook 2 minutes over low heat.

- Add cooking liquid and mushrooms to flour mixture. Stir well and cook 5 minutes over low heat.

- Add Gruyère and scallops. Stir and simmer 3 minutes over very low heat.

- Add hot pasta, stir and simmer another 3 minutes. Serve with grated Parmesan cheese.

1 SERVING			
Calories	493	Carbohydrate	51 g
Protein	41 g	Fat	12 g
Fiber	2 g		

Noodles with Tomato–Oyster Sauce

(4 servings)

¼ tsp	thyme	1 mL
½ tsp	basil	2 mL
¼ tsp	cayenne pepper	1 mL
½ tsp	fennel seed	2 mL
½ tsp	celery seed	2 mL
½ tsp	black pepper	2 mL
¼ tsp	ground ginger	1 mL
36	shucked oysters with their juice	36
2 tbsp	butter	30 mL
1	onion, chopped	1
3	green onions, chopped	3
½	green pepper, chopped	½
2 tbsp	chopped jalapeño pepper	30 mL
1	28-oz (796 mL) can tomatoes, drained and chopped	1
4	portions cooked noodles, hot	
	pinch of saffron	
	salt	

- Mix herbs and spices together and set aside.
- Pour oysters with their juice into a saucepan. Cover with cold water and poach 3 minutes over medium-low heat. Drain and set aside.
- Heat butter in a cast iron pan over medium heat. Add spice mixture, stir and cook 1 minute.
- Add onions, green pepper and jalapeño. Season with salt, stir and cook 4 minutes over medium heat. Stir in tomatoes and continue cooking 4 minutes. Season to taste with salt.
- Stir in drained oysters and simmer 3 to 4 minutes. Serve over noodles.

1 SERVING			
Calories	193	Carbohydrate	17 g
Protein	13 g	Fat	8 g
Fiber	2.9 g		

Shrimp Lafayette

(4 servings)

2 tbsp	butter	30 mL
1	onion, chopped	1
2	green peppers, chopped	2
1 tbsp	chopped jalapeño pepper	15 mL
4	tomatoes, peeled, seeded and chopped	4
2	garlic cloves, blanched, peeled and chopped	2
¼ tsp	cayenne pepper	1 mL
¼ tsp	black pepper	1 mL
¼ tsp	white pepper	1 mL
¼ tsp	brown sugar	1 mL
¼ cup	shrimp stock (see note)	50 mL
1¼ lb	fresh shrimp, peeled and deveined	625 g
4	portions cooked pasta, hot	
	salt	

- Heat 1 tbsp (15 mL) butter in a cast iron pan over medium heat. Add onion and both kind of peppers. Cook 10 minutes over low heat, stirring occasionally.

- Add tomatoes, garlic, spices and brown sugar. Stir well and cook 10 minutes over low heat.

- Incorporate shrimp stock and continue cooking 10 minutes, stirring occasionally. Remove from heat and set aside.

- Heat remaining butter in a frying pan over medium heat. Add shrimp and cook 3 to 4 minutes. Mix once during cooking.

- Add shrimp to tomato mixture, stir and let simmer 2 minutes over low heat. Serve over hot pasta.

●

Note: To make shrimp stock, pour 2 cups (500 mL) water into a saucepan. Add the shrimp shells and season with salt and pepper. Boil 15 minutes. Strain liquid before using.

1 SERVING			
Calories	272	Carbohydrate	11 g
Protein	40 g	Fat	8 g
Fiber	2.5 g		

Blackened Scallops

(4 servings)

1 tsp	oregano	5 mL
1 tsp	rosemary	5 mL
½ tsp	thyme	2 mL
1 tsp	paprika	5 mL
1 tsp	black pepper	5 mL
1 tsp	white pepper	5 mL
½ tsp	cayenne pepper	2 mL
1 tbsp	olive oil	15 mL
1	green pepper, diced	1
1	yellow pepper, diced	1
1	shallot, chopped	1
1 lb	scallops	500 g
4	small portions cooked pasta, hot	4
	salt	

- Mix herbs and spices, except salt, with oil in a small bowl; set aside.
- Heat a cast iron pan over high heat. When hot, add spice mixture to pan and cook 1 minute, stirring constantly.
- Add peppers and shallot; stir and cook 2 minutes over high heat.
- Add scallops. Stir well and cook 3 minutes over high heat. Stir once during cooking and season with salt.
- Serve over hot pasta. If desired, sprinkle with lemon juice.

1 SERVING			
Calories	336	Carbohydrate	42 g
Protein	31 g	Fat	5 g
Fiber	0 g		

Rigatoni with Fresh Clams and Tomatoes

(4 to 6 servings)

3 lb	fresh clams, scrubbed and washed	1.5 kg
½ cup	water	125 mL
2 tbsp	olive oil	30 mL
1	onion, chopped	1
1	shallot, chopped	1
3	garlic cloves, smashed and chopped	3
2 lb	tomatoes, peeled, seeded and cubed	1 kg
3 tbsp	tomato paste	45 mL
1 tsp	basil	5 mL
1 tsp	oregano	5 mL
4 to 6	portions cooked rigatoni, hot	4 to 6
	juice of 1 lemon	
	few drops of hot pepper sauce	
	salt and pepper	

- Place clams in a large saucepan. Add water and lemon juice. Cover and cook over medium heat until shells open. Discard any unopened clams.
- Remove clams from shells, chop and set aside.
- Strain cooking liquid from clams through a sieve lined with cheesecloth. Set liquid aside.
- Heat oil in a sauté pan over medium heat. Add onion, shallot and garlic. Cook 3 minutes over low heat.
- Add tomatoes, tomato paste and seasonings; bring to a boil. Reduce heat to low and cook 45 minutes. Stir a few times during cooking.
- Pour reserved cooking liquid from clams into a small saucepan. Cook 6 minutes over high heat.
- Incorporate ½ cup (125 mL) of the reduced cooking liquid into the tomato sauce. Continue cooking sauce 15 minutes over medium heat.
- Add chopped clams to tomato sauce and mix well. Simmer 3 minutes over low heat.
- Add pasta to sauce, stir and serve.

1 SERVING			
Calories	377	Carbohydrate	50 g
Protein	25 g	Fat	9 g
Fiber	3 g		

Creamy Curried Salmon

(4 servings)

2	salmon steaks, cooked	2
3 tbsp	butter	45 mL
1	onion, finely chopped	1
1	celery rib, sliced	1
½ lb	fresh mushrooms, cleaned and cut in three	250 g
2 tbsp	curry powder	30 mL
3 tbsp	all-purpose flour	45 mL
2½ cups	light chicken stock, heated	625 mL
3 tbsp	heavy cream	45 mL
2 tbsp	sherry	30 mL
4	portions cooked noodles, hot	4
	few drops of lemon juice	
	salt and pepper	

• Remove bones from salmon steaks. Flake salmon and set aside.

• Heat butter in a frying pan over medium heat. Add onion and celery; cook 3 minutes.

• Add mushrooms, season and stir in curry powder. Cook 4 minutes over low heat. Add flour, stir and cook 2 minutes.

• Pour in chicken stock and season. Cook 8 to 10 minutes over low heat. Incorporate cream and sherry. Add salmon and lemon juice. Stir and simmer 6 minutes over low heat.

• Serve with noodles.

1 SERVING			
Calories	283	Carbohydrate	7 g
Protein	22 g	Fat	18 g
Fiber	2 g		

Spaghettini with Zesty Anchovy Sauce

(4 servings)

1 tbsp	olive oil	15 mL
1	medium onion, finely chopped	1
2	garlic cloves, smashed and chopped	2
6	anchovy fillets, drained and chopped	6
4	tomatoes, peeled, seeded and chopped	4
½ tsp	finely chopped jalapeño pepper	2 mL
1 tbsp	basil	15 mL
1 lb	spaghettini, cooked al dente	500 g
	salt and pepper	
	grated cheese of your choice	

- Heat oil in a frying pan over medium heat. Add onion and garlic; cook 3 minutes. Add chopped anchovies, mixing well to combine.

- Add remaining ingredients, except pasta and cheese, and cook sauce 10 minutes over medium-low heat.

- Pour sauce over hot pasta and serve with grated cheese.

1 SERVING			
Calories	230	Carbohydrate	36 g
Protein	8 g	Fat	6 g
Fiber	4.6 g		

Jambalaya

(4 to 6 servings)

4	slices bacon, diced	4
1	large onion, finely diced	1
2	garlic cloves, smashed and chopped	2
4	tomatoes, peeled and chopped	4
½ tsp	fennel seed	2 mL
½ tsp	thyme	2 mL
1 cup	cooked rice	250 mL
1 cup	chicken stock, heated	250 mL
½ lb	cooked ham, cubed	250 g
¾ lb	shrimp, shelled, deveined and cooked	375 g
1	yellow pepper, cut in strips	1
1	green pepper, cut in strips	1
	few drops of hot pepper sauce	
	salt and pepper	

- Preheat oven to 350°F (180°C).
- Cook bacon in a large ovenproof frying pan over medium heat. When cooked, remove bacon using a slotted spoon and set aside.
- Add onion and garlic to hot pan. Cook 8 minutes over low heat, stirring occasionally. Stir in tomatoes, fennel seed and thyme. Cook 5 minutes.
- Add rice, chicken stock, ham and cooked bacon. Mix well and bring to a boil. Cover and cook 15 minutes in oven.
- Add shrimp and peppers to pan. Stir and add hot pepper sauce. Cover and return to oven; continue cooking 8 to 10 minutes before serving.

1 SERVING			
Calories	260	Carbohydrate	18 g
Protein	33 g	Fat	6 g
Fiber	2.2 g		

Seafood and Rice

(4 servings)

4 tbsp	olive oil	60 mL
1	onion, chopped	1
½	celery rib, finely diced	½
1 cup	long grain white rice, rinsed and drained	250 mL
1½ cups	light chicken or vegetable stock, heated	375 mL
½ lb	fresh shrimp, peeled and deveined	250 g
1 lb	fresh scallops, rinsed and dried	500 g
2	garlic cloves, peeled and sliced	2
1	zucchini, halved lengthwise and sliced	1
½ lb	fresh mushrooms, cleaned and sliced	250 g
	salt and pepper	
	soy sauce	
	lemon juice to taste	

- Preheat oven to 350°F (180°C).
- Heat 1 tbsp (15 mL) oil in an ovenproof casserole over medium heat. Add onion and celery; cook 2 minutes.
- Add rice, mix well and cook 2 minutes over high heat. Season generously.
- Pour in chicken stock, cover and cook 18 minutes in oven.
- About 8 minutes before the end of cooking, heat remaining oil in a frying pan over high heat. Add seafood and sauté 2 minutes, or according to size. Remove seafood from pan and set aside.
- Add garlic, zucchini and mushrooms to pan. Season well and cook 4 minutes over high heat.
- Return seafood to pan. Add soy sauce and lemon juice; mix well and season generously. Cook 1 minute, or according to size, and incorporate into rice. Mix with a fork and serve.

1 SERVING			
Calories	412	Carbohydrate	35 g
Protein	32 g	Fat	16 g
Fiber	4 g		

Shrimp

Steamed Shrimp

(4 servings)

2 cups	fish stock, heated (see page 18)	500 mL
½ tsp	fennel seed	2 mL
1 tsp	rosemary	5 mL
1½ lb	large fresh shrimp	750 g
1 tsp	black pepper	5 mL
	lemon juice	

- Pour fish stock into a saucepan. Add fennel and rosemary; cover and bring to a boil.
- Toss shrimp with black pepper. Place shrimp in a steamer basket (e.g. stainless steel, bamboo) and set in saucepan so that liquid does not touch the shrimp. Cover and cook 6 to 7 minutes. Stir shrimp in basket 2 to 3 times during cooking.
- Remove shrimp from basket and sprinkle with lemon juice. Serve.

1 SERVING			
Calories	200	Carbohydrate	0 g
Protein	45 g	Fat	2 g
Fiber	0 g		

Poached Paprika Shrimp

(4 servings)

3 tbsp	butter	45 mL
½ cup	water	125 mL
1½ lb	medium shrimp, peeled and deveined	750 g
1 tbsp	lemon juice	15 mL
2 tbsp	fresh tarragon	30 mL
1 tbsp	paprika	15 mL
	pepper	

- Heat butter and water in a sauté pan over medium heat. Bring to a boil and cook 2 minutes to melt butter completely.

- Reduce heat to low. Add shrimp and remaining ingredients; mix well. Cover with a sheet of waxed paper, laid on the surface of the food, and cook 5 minutes. Stir twice during cooking.

- Drain shrimp well and serve with lemon slices and cocktail sauce, if desired.

1 SERVING			
Calories	280	Carbohydrate	0 g
Protein	45 g	Fat	11 g
Fiber	0 g		

Shrimp and Spicy Italian Sausage Kebabs

(4 servings)

16	large shrimp, peeled and deveined	16
2	spicy Italian sausages, cut on the bias in ¾-inch (2 cm) thick pieces	2
2 tbsp	lemon juice	30 mL
½ cup	dry white wine	125 mL
2 tbsp	olive oil	30 mL
½ tsp	cayenne pepper	2 mL
½ tsp	black pepper	2 mL
3	large shallots, blanched and puréed	3
½ tsp	paprika	2 mL

- Place shrimp and sausages in a bowl.
- Mix remaining ingredients together, and then pour over shrimp and sausages. Marinate 1 hour.
- Preheat barbecue to medium.
- Alternate shrimp and pieces of sausage on skewers. Brush with marinade.
- Oil grill and place skewers on grill. Cover and cook 3 to 4 minutes on each side. Season to taste and baste with marinade during cooking. Serve.

1 SERVING

Calories	262	Carbohydrate	7 g
Protein	17 g	Fat	16 g
Fiber	0 g		

Shrimp with Caramelized Onions

(4 servings)

2 tbsp	olive oil	30 mL
4	onions, halved and sliced	4
2	garlic cloves, chopped	2
¼ cup	dry white wine	50 mL
½ cup	chicken stock	125 mL
1 tbsp	chopped fresh thyme	15 mL
1⅓ lb	fresh medium shrimp, peeled and deveined	650 g
	salt and freshly ground pepper	

• Heat oil in a medium saucepan over medium-low heat. Add onions and cook 10 minutes, or until onions are golden. Add garlic and white wine; continue cooking 3 minutes. Add chicken stock, season and cook 5 minutes.

• Add thyme and shrimp and cook 5 minutes over medium heat. Serve with steamed rice and sautéed rapini, if desired.

●

Note: Onions are low in calories and rich in sulfur and vitamin C. They may be difficult to digest when raw.

1 SERVING			
Calories	241	Carbohydrate	8 g
Protein	32 g	Fat	9 g
Fiber	1.3 g		

Cajun Shrimp on Skewers

(4 servings)

2	garlic cloves, blanched, peeled and puréed	2
½ tsp	cayenne pepper	2 mL
½ tsp	black pepper	2 mL
½ tsp	white pepper	2 mL
½ tsp	thyme	2 mL
1 tsp	oregano	5 mL
3 tbsp	melted butter	45 mL
¼ cup	shrimp stock (see Note on page 103)	50 mL
1¼ lb	shrimp, shelled and deveined	625 g
1	lemon, thinly sliced	1

- Mix garlic, spices, herbs and melted butter together in a small bowl; set aside.
- Pour shrimp stock into a bowl. Add spice mixture and shrimp. Mix well and let stand 15 minutes.
- Preheat grill to high.
- Alternate shrimp and slices of lemon on metal skewers. Baste with shrimp stock marinade.
- Oil grill and add shrimp skewers. Cook 3 minutes. Turn skewers over and cook 2 minutes. Baste with marinade during cooking.

1 SERVING			
Calories	247	Carbohydrate	2 g
Protein	37 g	Fat	10 g
Fiber	0 g		

Ginger Fried Shrimp

(4 servings)

1½ lb	fresh shrimp, peeled and deveined	750 g
3 tbsp	cornstarch	45 mL
1	large egg white, lightly beaten	1
2 tbsp	sherry	30 mL
4 tbsp	peanut oil	60 mL
2	green onions, sliced	2
1 oz	fresh ginger, julienned	30 g
1½ cups	fish stock or light chicken stock, heated	375 mL
1 cup	frozen green peas	250 mL
3 tbsp	cold water	45 mL
	salt and pepper	

- Place shrimp in a large bowl. Sprinkle in 2 tbsp (30 mL) cornstarch and mix well. Stir in egg white and sherry; season well.
- Heat oil in a large cast iron skillet over high heat. Add green onions and sliced ginger. Cook 30 seconds, remove from pan and set aside in a bowl.
- Divide shrimp into two batches. Cook each batch 3 minutes in skillet over high heat, stirring once. Season during cooking. Transfer shrimp to bowl with green onions and ginger.
- Add fish stock and peas to hot skillet. Dilute remaining cornstarch with cold water and add to liquid in pan. Mix well and cook 20 seconds. Pour over shrimp and serve.

1 SERVING			
Calories	414	Carbohydrate	20 g
Protein	41 g	Fat	18 g
Fiber	3 g		

Tasty Pepper Shrimp

(4 servings)

2	garlic cloves, puréed	2
½ tsp	cayenne pepper	2 mL
½ tsp	black pepper	2 mL
½ tsp	white pepper	2 mL
½ tsp	thyme	2 mL
1 tsp	oregano	5 mL
2 tbsp	butter	30 mL
¾ lb	fresh mushrooms, cleaned and cut in three	375 g
2	green onions, chopped	2
1½ lb	fresh shrimp, shelled and deveined	750 g
⅓ cup	shrimp stock (see Note on page 103)	75 mL
2 tbsp	beurre manié (see page 160)	30 mL
	salt	

- Grind garlic, peppers, thyme and oregano together with a mortar and pestle.
- Heat butter in a cast iron pan over medium heat. Add spice mixture and cook 1 minute.
- Add mushrooms and green onions. Season with salt, stir and cook 4 minutes.
- Add shrimp and cook 3 minutes. Stir once during cooking. Remove shrimp from pan and set aside.
- Increase heat to high and pour in shrimp stock. Bring to a boil and cook 2 minutes. Whisk in beurre manié.
- Return shrimp to pan and cook 1 minute over low heat. Serve over rice.

1 SERVING			
Calories	340	Carbohydrate	7 g
Protein	47 g	Fat	14 g
Fiber	2.6 g		

Sautéed Marinated Shrimp

(4 servings)

1 lb	shrimp, peeled and deveined	500 g
2	garlic cloves, smashed and chopped	2
2 tbsp	teriyaki sauce	30 mL
2 tbsp	olive oil	30 mL
1	large shallot, sliced	1
1	large zucchini, sliced	1
1	green pepper, sliced	1
¼ cup	slivered almonds	50 mL
	pinch of crushed chilies	
	juice of 1 lemon	
	salt and pepper	

- Place shrimp in a bowl. Add garlic, crushed chilies, teriyaki sauce and lemon juice. Marinate 30 minutes.

- Heat 1 tbsp (15 mL) oil in a frying pan over high heat. Add vegetables and season; cook 6 minutes. Remove vegetables from pan and set aside.

- Add remaining oil to pan and heat. Add shrimp and sauté 2 minutes on each side over high heat.

- Return vegetables to pan with shrimp. Pour in marinade and season well. Add almonds, stir and cook 2 minutes.

- Serve with rice.

1 SERVING			
Calories	298	Carbohydrate	12 g
Protein	34 g	Fat	13 g
Fiber	1.4 g		

Sauté of Shrimp and Potato

(4 servings)

2 tbsp	olive oil	30 mL
1 lb	medium shrimp, peeled, deveined and cut in two	500 g
2	medium potatoes, peeled and diced	2
½ lb	fresh mushrooms, cleaned and quartered	250 g
2	garlic cloves, smashed and chopped	2
1 tbsp	chopped fresh parsley	15 mL
1 tsp	chopped fresh fennel leaves	5 mL
	salt and pepper	

- Heat half the olive oil in a frying pan over high heat. Add shrimp and sauté 3 minutes. Remove from pan and set aside.

- Add remaining oil to hot pan. Add potatoes and season well; cook 4 minutes over medium heat. Mix well and cover pan; continue cooking 6 minutes or just until potatoes are almost cooked.

- Add mushrooms, garlic, parsley and fennel. Season and cook 4 minutes over high heat.

- Return shrimp to pan, mix and cook 2 minutes to reheat. Serve.

1 SERVING			
Calories	301	Carbohydrate	23 g
Protein	33 g	Fat	9 g
Fiber	1.6 g		

Richmond Shrimp Sauté

(4 servings)

1 tbsp	olive oil	15 mL
1¼ lb	fresh shrimp, shelled and deveined	625 g
2	medium beets, cooked and quartered	2
1 cup	cooked corn	250 mL
2	garlic cloves, smashed and chopped	2
1 tbsp	chopped fresh tarragon	15 mL
1	avocado, cut in wedges	1
1 tsp	chopped fresh parsley	5 mL
	juice of 1 lemon	
	salt and pepper	

- Heat oil in a frying pan over high heat. Add shrimp and season well; cook 2 minutes.
- Turn shrimp over and continue cooking 2 to 3 minutes. Remove shrimp from pan and set aside.
- Add beets, corn and garlic to hot pan. Cook 1 minute over high heat. Return shrimp to pan and season. Add tarragon and cook 2 minutes.
- Serve shrimp and vegetables garnished with wedges of avocado. Sprinkle with lemon juice and chopped parsley.

1 SERVING			
Calories	334	Carbohydrate	20 g
Protein	40 g	Fat	10 g
Fiber	3.7 g		

Crêpes for Seafood

(4 servings)

1 cup	all-purpose flour	250 mL
3	large eggs	3
1 cup	milk	250 mL
½ cup	water	125 mL
2 tbsp	vegetable oil	30 mL
	pinch salt	
	butter	

- Place flour and salt in a large bowl. Add eggs and mix well with a wooden spoon.
- Whisk in milk and water. If batter is too thick, add more water. Whisk in oil and strain batter into a clean bowl.
- Cover with plastic wrap laid directly on the surface of the batter. Refrigerate 1 hour.
- Bring batter to room temperature before using. If too thick, add more milk.

- Place a crêpe pan over medium heat. When hot, use a paper towel to wipe pan with butter. Pour out excess butter.
- Add a ladle of crêpe batter and, holding pan above stove, rotate to spread batter evenly. Turn pan on a 90 degree angle and let excess batter drip back into bowl.
- Return pan to stove and cook crêpe over medium-high heat until underside is golden brown. Using a long metal spatula, turn crêpe over carefully and cook other side.
- Remove pan from heat and let crêpe slide out onto a large dinner plate.
- Add more butter to pan, heat and repeat process. Stack crêpes on plate.

1 SERVING			
Calories	278	Carbohydrate	28 g
Protein	10 g	Fat	14 g
Fiber	1 g		

Shrimp and White Sauce Crêpes

(4 servings)

3 tbsp	butter	45 mL
2	shallots, chopped	2
1 lb	fresh shrimp, peeled, deveined and halved	500 g
½ lb	fresh mushrooms, cleaned and sliced	250 g
3 tbsp	all-purpose flour	45 mL
2 cups	milk, heated	500 mL
1 tbsp	chopped fresh chives	15 mL
8	crêpes	8
¼ cup	grated Parmesan cheese	50 mL
	salt and pepper	
	paprika and nutmeg	

- Heat butter in a frying pan over medium heat. Add shallots and shrimp. Season well and cook 2 to 3 minutes. Remove shrimp and set aside.
- Add mushrooms to pan and increase heat to high. Cook 4 minutes.
- Sprinkle in flour and mix well. Pour in milk and add all seasonings. Whisk thoroughly and cook 6 minutes over low heat.
- Remove pan from heat and incorporate shrimp. Divide half of mixture between crêpes, roll and place in a baking dish. Top with remaining sauce and cheese; broil 4 minutes in oven. Serve.

1 SERVING			
Calories	429	Carbohydrate	27 g
Protein	33 g	Fat	21 g
Fiber	2.3 g		

OTHER Seafood

Marinated Scallop and Vegetable Brochettes

(4 servings)

MARINADE

1 cup	dry white wine	250 mL
1	shallot, chopped	1
2 tbsp	olive oil	30 mL
2	garlic cloves, sliced	2
1 tsp	chopped fresh parsley	5 mL
1 tsp	chopped fresh tarragon	5 mL
1 tsp	chopped fresh basil	5 mL
1 tsp	chopped fresh oregano	5 mL
1½ lb	fresh scallops, rinsed	750 g
	salt and pepper	
	lemon juice	

BROCHETTES

2	large carrots, pared and sliced ½-inch (1-cm) thick	2
¼	head broccoli, cut in bite-size pieces	¼
½ lb	fresh mushroom caps, cleaned	250 g
	salt and pepper	

- Place all marinade ingredients, except scallops, in a bowl and mix well. Add scallops and cover with plastic wrap laid on the surface of marinade. Refrigerate 1 hour. Remove scallops and reserve marinade.

- Blanch carrots and broccoli separately in salted, boiling water. Drain well and pat dry with paper towels.

- Alternate scallops, mushroom caps, carrots and broccoli on metal skewers. Baste with marinade and season generously. Broil 4 to 5 minutes in oven, rotating 2 or 3 times during cooking. Baste frequently with marinade.

- Sprinkle with lemon juice and serve on a bed of rice.

1 SERVING

Calories	211	Carbohydrate	14 g
Protein	32 g	Fat	3 g
Fiber	3.5 g		

Tossed Vegetables with Sea Scallops

(4 servings)

3 tbsp	olive oil	45 mL
1½ lb	scallops, rinsed, drained and dried	750 g
1	onion, sliced	1
2 cups	cooked spinach, drained and chopped	500 mL
2	carrots, sliced	2
1	yellow pepper, sliced	1
1 cup	frozen green peas	250 mL
1½ cups	fish stock or clam juice	375 mL
¼ tsp	fennel seed	1 mL
2 tsp	cornstarch	10 mL
3 tbsp	cold water	45 mL
	salt and pepper	
	cayenne pepper	

- Heat 2 tbsp (30 mL) oil in a large frying pan over high heat. Add scallops and cook 2 to 3 minutes, browning both sides. Season well, remove with a slotted spoon and set aside.

- Add vegetables, except peas, to pan. Season well and cook 5 minutes over high heat. Add peas, fish stock or clam juice, and fennel seed. Simmer 3 minutes and season with cayenne pepper to taste.

- Dilute cornstarch in cold water; incorporate into mixture. Return scallops to pan, season well and simmer 2 minutes. Serve.

1 SERVING

Calories	378	Carbohydrate	28 g
Protein	35 g	Fat	14 g
Fiber	7.4 g		

Charleston-Style Scallops

(4 servings)

1	shallot, finely chopped	1
1 lb	fresh mushrooms, cleaned and quartered	500 g
1¼ lb	fresh scallops, washed	625 g
1 tbsp	chopped fresh parsley	15 mL
1 cup	dry white wine	250 mL
¼ cup	water	50 mL
¼ tsp	paprika	1 mL
2 tbsp	butter	30 mL
3 tbsp	all-purpose flour	45 mL
1 cup	grated Gruyère cheese	250 mL
	juice of 1 lemon	
	salt and pepper	

- Place shallot, mushrooms, scallops and parsley in a sauté pan. Do not mix. Add wine, lemon juice and water. Season with salt, pepper and paprika. Stir gently and cover with a sheet of waxed paper, laid on the surface of the food. Bring to a boil over medium heat.

- As soon as liquid starts to boil, remove pan from heat. Let stand 2 minutes.

- Using a slotted spoon, remove scallops from pan and set aside in a bowl.

- Return pan to stove and cook mushrooms and liquid 4 minutes over high heat.

- Melt butter in a saucepan over medium heat. Add flour and mix well; cook 2 minutes over low heat.

- Pour mushrooms and cooking liquid from scallops into flour mixture in saucepan. Mix well and cook sauce 10 minutes over low heat.

- Stir scallops into mushroom sauce. Transfer mixture to an ovenproof baking dish and top with cheese. Broil in oven 4 minutes to brown. Serve.

1 SERVING			
Calories	454	Carbohydrate	19 g
Protein	46 g	Fat	17 g
Fiber	3.4 g		

Steamed Mussels with Curry

(4 servings)

5 lb	large mussels, bearded and scrubbed	2.5 kg
5 tbsp	butter	75 mL
2	shallots, chopped	2
2	fresh fennel sprigs	2
2	fresh parsley sprigs	2
1 cup	dry white wine	250 mL
1	onion, chopped	1
1 tbsp	curry powder	15 mL
1 cup	heavy cream	250 mL
2 tbsp	chopped fresh parsley	30 mL
	lemon juice	
	salt and pepper	

- Place mussels, 4 tbsp (60 mL) butter, shallots, herb sprigs, wine and lemon juice in a large saucepan. Season with pepper.

- Cover and cook over low heat until shells open, about 5 minutes. Shake pan several times during cooking to mix mussels.

- Remove mussels from pan, discarding any unopened mussels, and keep warm. Strain liquid through a sieve lined with cheesecloth; set aside.

- Heat remaining butter in a saucepan. Add onion and curry powder, and cook 5 minutes over medium heat. Add reserved cooking liquid, increase heat to high and bring to a boil.

- Add cream and parsley; season well and cook 4 minutes.

- Return mussels to saucepan, simmer 2 minutes and serve immediately.

1 SERVING			
Calories	833	Carbohydrate	26 g
Protein	67 g	Fat	49 g
Fiber	0.5 g		

Fresh Mussels

(4 servings)

9 lb	mussels, washed and scrubbed	4.5 kg
1 cup	dry white wine	250 mL
2	fresh parsley sprigs	2
2	shallots, chopped	2
1 tsp	fennel seed	5 mL
½ cup	fish stock (see page 18) or water	125 mL
1 tbsp	beurre manié (see page 160)	15 mL
1 tbsp	chopped fresh parsley	15 mL
	salt and pepper	

- Place mussels in a large saucepan. Add wine, pepper, parsley sprigs, shallots, fennel seed and fish stock. Cover and cook 10 to 12 minutes over medium heat or just until shells open. Shake pan 2 to 3 times during cooking.

- When mussels open, remove from pan and place in a bowl. Set aside. Discard any unopened mussels.

- Line a sieve with cheesecloth and strain cooking liquid into a clean saucepan. Season with salt and pepper. Stir in beurre manié and chopped parsley. Cook 3 minutes over high heat, whisking constantly.

- Pour sauce over mussels and serve.

1 SERVING			
Calories	461	Carbohydrate	21 g
Protein	73 g	Fat	5 g
Fiber	0 g		

Steamed Mussels with Cream Sauce

(4 servings)

5 lb	fresh mussels, bearded and scrubbed	2.5 kg
5 tbsp	butter	75 mL
3	shallots, chopped	3
2 cups	dry white wine	500 mL
1 cup	heavy cream	250 mL
1 tbsp	chopped fresh parsley	15 mL
	salt and pepper	

• Place mussels in a large saucepan. Add 3 tbsp (45 mL) butter, shallots, wine and pepper.

• Cover and bring to a boil. Cook mussels over low heat until shells open, about 5 minutes. Shake pan several times during cooking to mix mussels.

• Remove mussels from pan, discarding any unopened mussels; keep warm. Strain liquid through a sieve lined with cheesecloth, into a saucepan. Cook liquid over medium heat until reduced by a third.

• Add cream and remaining butter. Cook 4 minutes over low heat. Stir in parsley and correct seasoning.

• Return mussels to large saucepan and pour in cream sauce. Simmer several minutes and serve.

1 SERVING			
Calories	844	Carbohydrate	24 g
Protein	67 g	Fat	49 g
Fiber	0 g		

Seafood Casserole

(4 servings)

¾ lb	large scallops	375 g
¾ lb	shrimp, peeled and deveined	375 g
½ tsp	fennel seed	2 mL
1 tbsp	chopped fresh parsley	15 mL
½ cup	dry white wine	125 mL
1½ cups	clam juice	375 mL
4 tbsp	butter	60 mL
½ lb	fresh mushrooms, cleaned and chopped	250 g
2	shallots, chopped	2
3 tbsp	all-purpose flour	45 mL
3 tbsp	bread crumbs	45 mL
	salt and pepper	

- Place scallops and shrimp in a sauté pan. Add fennel seed, parsley, wine and clam juice. Season with salt and pepper. Cover with a sheet of waxed paper, laid on the surface of the food. Place on stove and bring just to boiling point over medium heat. Do not allow liquid to boil. Remove sauté pan from heat and let stand 4 minutes.

- Remove seafood from liquid and set aside. Place sauté pan over medium heat and cook liquid 4 minutes.

- Heat 3 tbsp (45 mL) butter in another frying pan over medium heat. Add mushrooms and shallots. Season well and cook 4 minutes. Mix in flour and cook 1 minute.

- Pour in reserved cooking liquid and mix well. Cook 4 minutes.

- Slice seafood on the bias. Transfer to a baking dish and cover with the mushroom sauce.

- Preheat oven to broil.

- Mix remaining butter with bread crumbs; sprinkle over casserole. Broil 3 minutes in oven and serve.

1 SERVING			
Calories	416	Carbohydrate	19 g
Protein	48 g	Fat	15 g
Fiber	2.1 g		

Seafood in Pastry

(4 servings)

2	sole fillets	2
1 lb	small scallops, rinsed	500 g
½ lb	fresh mushrooms, cleaned and sliced	250 g
2	shallots, chopped	2
1½	red peppers, thinly sliced	1½
1	fresh fennel sprig	1
2	fresh parsley sprigs	2
1 cup	dry white wine	250 mL
3 tbsp	butter	45 mL
3 tbsp	all-purpose flour	45 mL
4	small vol-au-vent pastry shells	4
	salt and pepper	
	lemon juice to taste	

- Place fillets in a large frying pan. Add scallops, mushrooms, shallots, peppers, herbs and wine. Cover with cold water and season well.

- Cover with a sheet of waxed paper, laid on the surface of the food. Bring to a boil over medium heat. Remove immediately from heat and let stand 2 minutes.

- Using a slotted spoon, remove seafood and set aside. Reserve cooking liquid and vegetables; discard herb sprigs.

- Heat butter in a saucepan over medium heat. Sprinkle in flour and mix well; cook 20 seconds. Incorporate reserved cooking liquid and vegetables. Season and cook 4 minutes.

- Meanwhile, heat pastry shells in a warm oven.

- Add seafood to sauce and simmer 2 minutes over low heat. Sprinkle with lemon juice and fill vol-au-vents with mixture. Serve.

1 SERVING			
Calories	362	Carbohydrate	18 g
Protein	31 g	Fat	14 g
Fiber	2.3 g		

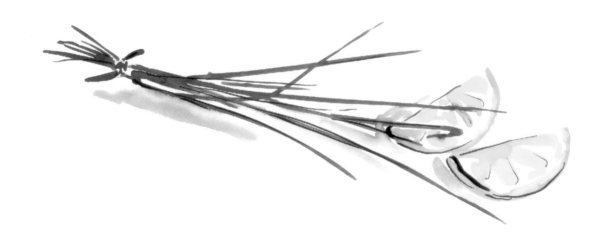

Lobster Newburg

(4 servings)

1½ cups	dry white wine	375 mL
½ cup	clam juice or fish stock	125 mL
2	1½ lb (750 g) boiled lobsters	2
4 tbsp	butter	60 mL
4	shallots, chopped	4
¾ lb	fresh mushrooms, cleaned and diced	375 g
2 tbsp	all-purpose flour	30 mL
1 cup	light cream, heated	250 mL
¼ cup	Madeira wine	50 mL
	salt and pepper	
	paprika	
	chopped fresh parsley	

- Bring white wine to a boil in a saucepan and cook 3 minutes. Add clam juice and reduce heat to low. Simmer until ready to use.

- Cut lobsters in half. Discard intestinal sac. Scoop out any tomalley and coral and reserve in a small bowl. Remove lobster meat from shells and dice large; set aside.

- Clean shells and dry in a warm oven.

- Heat butter in a frying pan over medium heat. Add lobster, shallots, pepper and paprika. Cook 2 minutes over high heat. Remove lobster from pan and set aside.

- Add mushrooms to pan and season well. Cook 4 minutes over medium heat. Sprinkle in flour and mix well; cook 2 minutes.

- Incorporate simmering wine mixture to mushrooms. Mix well and pour in cream. Season, stir and cook sauce 6 minutes over low heat.

- Stir in reserved tomalley and coral. Return lobster to pan and stir in Madeira wine. Season well and simmer 4 minutes.

- Fill lobster shells with mixture and sprinkle with parsley. Serve.

1 SERVING			
Calories	557	Carbohydrate	18 g
Protein	72 g	Fat	21 g
Fiber	1.6 g		

Lobster à la Bretonne

(4 servings)

BEURRE MANIÉ (KNEADED BUTTER)		
5 tbsp	butter, softened	75 mL
2 tbsp	all-purpose flour	30 mL
LOBSTER		
4	live lobsters, each 1½ lb (750 g)	4
3 tbsp	butter	45 mL
2	shallots, chopped	2
2	garlic cloves, smashed and chopped	2
2	fresh tarragon sprigs	2
3 tbsp	cognac	45 mL
½ cup	dry white wine	125 mL
1½ cups	fish stock, heated (see page 18)	375 mL
3 tbsp	beurre manié	45 mL
3 tbsp	heavy cream	45 mL
	Tabasco sauce	
	salt and pepper	

- Blend butter with flour to make the beurre manié. Set aside.
- Place lobsters in a large pot filled with boiling, salted water. Boil 1 minute over high heat. Remove lobsters and drain. Set aside to cool.
- Place lobsters right-side up on counter and hold with one hand. Spread tail flat on counter. Cut off claws.
- Cut lobster bodies into large pieces. Discard gravel sac in head and intestinal sac in tail. Remove tomalley and reserve in a bowl.
- Heat butter in a frying pan. Add shallots, garlic and tarragon. Cook 1 minute.
- Add lobster pieces and claws. Season with salt and pepper; cook 2 minutes over high heat. Cover and continue cooking just until lobster shells become red in color.
- Add cognac and flambé. Remove lobster pieces from pan and set aside.
- Pour white wine into pan and cook 3 minutes over high heat. Incorporate fish stock and continue cooking 4 minutes over high heat.
- Stir in beurre manié and continue cooking to thicken sauce. Whisk constantly.
- Mix cream with reserved tomalley. Stir into sauce and add a few drops of Tabasco sauce. Cook 3 minutes over medium heat.
- Place lobster pieces in sauce and simmer 2 minutes. Serve.

1 SERVING			
Calories	605	Carbohydrate	8 g
Protein	71 g	Fat	27 g
Fiber	0 g		

Poached Lobster in Lemon Garlic Butter

(4 servings)

4	live lobsters, 1¼ lb (625 g) each	4
1 cup	butter	250 mL
2	garlic cloves, finely chopped	2
2 tbsp	chopped fresh parsley	30 mL
	lemon juice	

- Plunge lobsters into a stockpot filled with boiling water. Cook 12 to 14 minutes over medium heat; do not let water resume full boil.

- As soon as lobsters are cooked, remove from pot and drain well.

- Melt butter in a small saucepan; add garlic, parsley and lemon juice to taste. Serve lobster with garlic butter and steamed rice, if desired.

1 SERVING			
Calories	567	Carbohydrate	1 g
Protein	26 g	Fat	51 g
Fiber	0.2 g		

Crab and Eggplant Coquilles

(4 to 6 servings)

2	eggplants	2
2 tbsp	butter	30 mL
1	onion, finely chopped	1
1	yellow pepper, chopped	1
2 tbsp	chopped jalapeño pepper	30 mL
2	garlic cloves, smashed and chopped	2
¼ tsp	cayenne pepper	1 mL
¼ tsp	black pepper	1 mL
½ tsp	fennel seed	2 mL
7 oz	crabmeat, thawed if frozen	200 g
½ cup	grated Parmesan cheese	125 mL
	salt and pepper	

1 SERVING

Calories	141	Carbohydrate	6 g
Protein	11 g	Fat	8 g
Fiber	1.5 g		

- Cut eggplants in half lengthwise and sprinkle flesh with salt. Let stand 30 minutes at room temperature. Rinse under cold water to remove salt and juices.

- Preheat oven to 400°F (200°C).

- Pat eggplants dry and arrange, flesh-side up, in a roasting pan. Bake 30 minutes. Remove from oven and scoop out eggplant to form shells, reserving removed eggplant. Set aside.

- Heat butter in a cast iron pan over medium heat. Add onion, yellow pepper, jalapeño pepper and garlic. Stir and cook 3 minutes.

- Add spices, stir and cook 2 minutes. Mix in reserved eggplant flesh. Season and cook 6 to 7 minutes.

- Stir in crabmeat; correct seasoning. Add 3 tbsp (45 mL) Parmesan, stir and cook 4 minutes over low heat.

- Fill eggplant shells or coquille dishes with mixture. Top with remaining cheese and cook 8 minutes in oven at 350°F (180°C).

Scampi with Julienne of Vegetables

(4 servings)

3 tbsp	olive oil	45 mL
24	large scampi, peeled, deveined and halved	24
8	green onions, cut in 1-inch (2.5 cm) lengths	8
2	large carrots, pared and julienned	2
½ lb	fresh mushroom caps, cleaned	250 g
½ lb	green beans, pared, cooked and halved	250 g
3	garlic cloves, peeled and sliced	3
2 tbsp	chopped fresh basil	30 mL
1 tbsp	chopped fresh parsley	15 mL
	salt and pepper	
	lemon juice	

- Heat 2 tbsp (30 mL) oil in a frying pan over high heat. Add scampi and sauté 2 minutes. Remove from pan and set aside.
- Add remaining oil to pan. Cook remaining ingredients 5 minutes over high heat.
- Return scampi to pan, mix well and cook 2 minutes.
- Sprinkle with more lemon juice and serve over white rice.

1 SERVING			
Calories	292	Carbohydrate	17 g
Protein	29 g	Fat	12 g
Fiber	3.8 g		

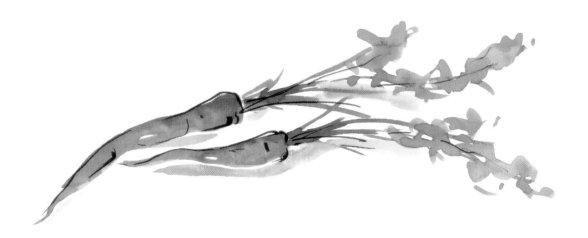

Scampi au Gratin

(4 servings)

GARLIC BUTTER

½ lb	soft butter	250 g
1	shallot, finely chopped	1
2	garlic cloves, finely chopped	2
1 tsp	chopped fresh parsley	5 mL
	pepper	
	lemon juice to taste	

SCAMPI

16	large scampi	16
⅔ cup	white bread crumbs	150 mL
	pepper	
	lemon wedges	

• Mix the ingredients for the garlic butter together in a bowl and set aside.

• Preheat oven to 425°F (220°C).

• Place scampi shell-side up on a cutting board. Using a sharp knife, cut lengthwise through shell, leaving enough flesh intact to open butterfly-style. Devein.

• Wash under cold water, drain and pat dry with paper towels.

• Place scampi, flesh-side up, on ovenproof tray. Season with pepper and spread with garlic butter to taste.

• Top with bread crumbs. Cook 4 minutes in oven. Change oven setting to broil and brown several minutes.

• Serve with lemon wedges.

1 SERVING

Calories	543	Carbohydrate	13 g
Protein	17 g	Fat	47 g
Fiber	0 g		

Asian Dishes

Sushi Rice

(4 cups/1 L)

2 cups	short grain sushi rice	500 mL
2¼ cups	water	550 mL
1	3-inch (7.5 cm) square kombu seaweed	1
4 tbsp	sake or mirin (rice wine)	60 mL
4 tbsp	rice vinegar	60 mL
2 tbsp	sugar	30 mL
2 tsp	sea salt	10 mL

• Rinse rice under cold running water for 20 minutes. Drain well and place rice in a heavy saucepan; add water, kombu and sake. Bring to a boil, remove kombu and reduce heat to low. Cover and cook about 15 minutes, or until all the liquid has been absorbed. Do not stir during cooking.

• Remove pan from heat and let cool 15 minutes. Using a wooden spoon, gently stir rice. Cover with a towel and let stand 10 minutes.

• Combine vinegar, sugar and salt and pour over rice. Toss rice gently until it cools to room temperature. Cover with a damp towel and set aside at room temperature until ready to use.

Maki Sushi

(4 servings)

4	sheets nori seaweed	4
1 cup	cooked sushi rice	250 mL
1½ oz	fresh salmon	45 g
2½ oz	fresh tuna	75 g
2½ oz	fresh crabmeat	75 g
	strips of avocado, green onion, cucumber, red and yellow pepper	
	soy sauce	
	marinated ginger slices	
	wasabi paste (see Note on page 175)	

• Use a whole sheet or a ½ sheet of seaweed, depending on the size of rolls desired. Place the sheet on a makisu (bamboo mat). Wet the tips of your fingers and spread rice over seaweed, leaving a 1-inch (2.5 cm) border at each end.

• Place desired fish and garnishes in center, and roll using the makisu. Press down to seal. Repeat with remaining nori. Slice the rolls with a wet knife. Serve with soy sauce, marinated ginger and wasabi.

●

Note: Nori seaweed is rich in calcium, phosphorous, iron, iodine and vitamin A. It is compressed into speckled sheets, ranging in color from brown to dark green.

1 SERVING			
Calories	194	Carbohydrate	22 g
Protein	13 g	Fat	6 g
Fiber	0.3 g		

Nigiri Sushi

(4 servings)

2½ cups	cooked sushi rice (see page 172)	625 mL
1	sheet nori seaweed	1
4 tbsp	salmon roe	60 mL
8	large shrimp, cooked and peeled	8
⅓ lb	fresh red tuna, cut into 8 strips	150 g
⅓ lb	fresh bonito, cut into 8 strips	150 g
1	green onion, thinly sliced	1
1 tbsp	wasabi powder	15 mL
	marinated ginger slices	
	soy sauce	
	black radish sprouts	

- Moisten hands and mold 2 tbsp (30 mL) sushi rice into an oval shaped ball. You should be able to make 28 balls in all.
- Cut nori sheet into 1 x 7-inch (2.5 x 17.5 cm) rectangles. Roll each rectangle around a ball of rice. The seaweed should come up a bit higher than the rice so that you can top the rice with 1 tbsp (15 mL) salmon roe.
- Place 1 strip of fish or shrimp on each of the remaining balls of rice. Press gently but firmly to keep the fish in place. Garnish with green onion.
- Mix wasabi powder with enough hot water to make a thick paste. Serve nigiri sushi with wasabi paste, marinated ginger slices and soy sauce. Accompany with black radish sprouts.

●

Note: Wasabi is a root that is part of the horseradish family. It has a strong flavor and is served with sushi and sashimi. Dried and ground, it is sold either as a powder or a paste. It is sold fresh only in Japan.

1 SERVING			
Calories	338	Carbohydrate	43 g
Protein	28 g	Fat	6 g
Fiber	1.2 g		

Sashimi

(4 servings)

⅓ lb	daikon radish, julienned	150 g
⅓ lb	carrots, julienned	150 g
1 tbsp	wasabi powder	15 mL
½ lb	yellowtail tuna fillets, cut in 12 pieces	225 g
½ lb	salmon fillets, cut in 12 pieces	225 g
½ lb	mackerel fillets, cut in 12 pieces	225 g
	lettuce leaves	
	marinated ginger slices	
	soy sauce	

- Soak daikon and carrot in very cold water for 1 hour.
- Mix wasabi powder with enough hot water to make a thick paste.
- Place 3 pieces of each kind of fish on each of 4 plates. Drain daikon and carrot well, and divide among plates, along with lettuce. Serve with wasabi paste, marinated ginger and soy sauce.

Note: Ginger marinated with vinegar is the essential Japanese condiment for sushi. It is eaten between courses, to clean the palate and freshen the breath. It also has certain antibiotic properties.

1 SERVING			
Calories	199	Carbohydrate	6 g
Protein	37 g	Fat	3 g
Fiber	2.1 g		

Shrimp, Fish and Vegetable Tempura

(4 servings)

2	eggs	2
1¾ cups	cold water	425 mL
¼ tsp	salt	1 mL
2 cups	all-purpose flour	500 mL
8 oz	turbot fillets, cut into strips	250 g
8 oz	bonito fillets, cut into strips	250 g
8	large shrimp	8
2	carrots, sliced diagonally	2
1	zucchini, sliced diagonally	1
8	flat green beans, sliced in three	8
	soy sauce and dashi	
	peanut oil for deep-frying	
DASHI		
8 cups	water	2 L
⅓ oz	dried bonito flakes	10 g
½	kombu seaweed	½

- Preheat peanut oil in a deep-fryer to 340°F (170°C).
- Beat eggs and stir in cold water with chopsticks. Add salt and gradually stir in flour. Do not mix too much or batter will become sticky.
- Rinse the fish and pat dry with paper towels; season well. Dip strips in batter and deep-fry in hot oil. Repeat with shrimp, carrots, zucchini and green beans. Tempura is ready when it rises to the surface and is lightly golden.
- Carefully remove from oil and drain on paper towels. Serve with a mixture of equal parts soy sauce and dashi.
- To make the dashi, bring water to a boil in a large saucepan. Add bonito flakes and kombu seaweed. Cook over medium heat a few seconds, or until bonito flakes sink to the bottom. Strain through cheesecloth.

●

Note: Tempura is a Japanese technique for preparing fish and vegetable fritters. The oil is too hot when the fritters rise immediately to the surface. If the fritters stay on the bottom of the fryer, the oil is not hot enough.

1 SERVING			
Calories	713	Carbohydrate	57 g
Protein	38 g	Fat	37 g
Fiber	3.8 g		

Shrimp Fritters with Coriander

(4 servings)

½ lb	shrimp, peeled and deveined	225 g
1 cup	all-purpose flour	250 mL
4 tbsp	chopped fresh coriander	60 mL
3	garlic cloves, chopped	3
2 tbsp	chopped fresh ginger	30 mL
1	egg	1
¾ cup	coconut cream	175 mL
	salt and freshly ground pepper	
	peanut oil for deep-frying	
	soy sauce	
	alfalfa sprouts	

- Preheat peanut oil in a deep-fryer to 350°F (180°C).
- Finely chop shrimp and place in a bowl. Add flour, coriander, garlic and ginger; mix well. Beat egg and add coconut cream. Pour into shrimp mixture; season and mix well.
- Deep-fry spoonfuls of mixture in hot oil for about 5 minutes, or until fritters are golden and puffy.
- Serve with soy sauce and alfalfa sprouts.

●

Note: Because eggs absorb odors, it is important to keep them in a cardboard or plastic container in the refrigerator.

1 SERVING			
Calories	495	Carbohydrate	30 g
Protein	15 g	Fat	35 g
Fiber	1.1 g		

Red Snapper and Spinach Wontons

(4 servings)

1 tbsp	vegetable oil	15 mL
2	shallots, chopped	2
2 cups	chopped fresh spinach	500 mL
½ lb	red snapper fillets, diced	225 g
½ lb	crabmeat	225 g
2 tbsp	soy sauce	30 mL
1 tbsp	brown sugar	15 mL
1 lb	wonton wrappers	450 g
	freshly ground pepper	
	peanut oil for deep-frying	

- Heat vegetable oil in a medium-sized frying pan and sauté shallots 2 minutes over low heat. Add spinach and cook 1 minute or until wilted. Place in a medium bowl. Add snapper, crabmeat, soy sauce, brown sugar and pepper to taste; mix well.

- Preheat peanut oil in deep-fryer to 350°F (180°C).

- Place 1 tbsp (15 mL) of fish filling on each wrapper. Brush edges with water and fold corners in, pressing together to seal.

- Fry wontons in hot oil until golden.

- Serve with a hot chili pepper sauce, or sauce of your choice.

1 SERVING			
Calories	563	Carbohydrate	34 g
Protein	28 g	Fat	35 g
Fiber	3.5 g		

Japanese Salmon and Tofu Balls

¾ lb	salmon fillets	350 g
½ lb	tofu	225 g
¼ cup	all-purpose flour	50 mL
2 tbsp	chopped fresh garlic chives	30 mL
¼ cup	soy sauce	50 mL
	marinated ginger slices	
	salt and freshly ground pepper	
	peanut oil for deep-frying	
	extra flour for coating	

- Place salmon in a medium saucepan and cover with salted water. Bring to a boil over medium-high heat. Reduce heat and simmer about 3 minutes. Drain; remove skin and bones. Flake salmon and chop fine.

- Cut tofu into ½-inch (1 cm) squares and cook 2 minutes in salted, boiling water. Drain well and transfer to a clean piece of cheesecloth; squeeze to remove excess liquid. Place tofu in a bowl and mash with a fork. Add salmon, flour and garlic chives. Season and mix well.

- Preheat oil in deep-fryer to 350°F (180°C).

- Form salmon mixture into balls. Roll in flour and deep-fry in hot oil until golden. Serve with soy sauce and marinated ginger.

●

Note: Tofu (or bean curd) is made from soy beans that are first soaked and puréed and then boiled and sieved. Soaked in water, it will keep 5 days in the refrigerator. The water should be changed daily.

1 SERVING			
Calories	344	Carbohydrate	9 g
Protein	23 g	Fat	24 g
Fiber	1 g		

Crab Spring Rolls with Sweet and Sour Sauce

(4 servings)

SWEET AND SOUR SAUCE

4 tbsp	brown sugar	60 mL
4 tbsp	rice vinegar	60 mL
½ cup	chicken broth	125 mL
2 tbsp	soy sauce	30 mL
2 tbsp	fish sauce (nam pla)	30 mL
1 tbsp	chopped fresh ginger	15 mL
1 tbsp	tomato paste	15 mL
1 tbsp	cornstarch	15 mL
2 tbsp	water	30 mL

SPRING ROLLS

½ lb	crabmeat	225 g
1 cup	bean sprouts	250 mL
2	carrots, julienned	2
2	garlic cloves, finely chopped	2
1 tbsp	fish sauce (nam pla)	15 mL
2 tbsp	chopped fresh lemon basil	30 mL
2 tbsp	chopped fresh mint	30 mL
8	rice paper wrappers (7 inch/17.5 cm in diameter)	8
	peanut oil for deep-frying	
	fresh spinach and julienned carrots	

- In a small saucepan, mix together all sauce ingredients, except cornstarch and water, and bring to a boil. Dilute cornstarch in the water; add to sauce and cook about 3 minutes.
- In a medium bowl, mix together crabmeat, bean sprouts, carrots, garlic, fish sauce, basil and mint. Set filling aside.
- Preheat oil in deep-fryer to 375°F (190°C).
- Dip a rice paper wrapper in hot water for 20 seconds, or until it is soft. Spread out on work surface and place a small amount of filling in the center. Fold wrapper over the filling and fold in ends before rolling. Repeat with the other wrappers.
- Deep-fry rolls in hot oil until they are crispy and lightly golden. Serve with sweet and sour sauce, alongside the fresh spinach and julienned carrot.

●

Note: Rice paper wrappers are made with flour, salt and water, mixed into a paste. They are cooked between hot irons and dried.

1 SERVING			
Calories	304	Carbohydrate	33 g
Protein	16 g	Fat	12 g
Fiber	1.6 g		

FOR Fish Lovers

Salmon en Papillote with Basil Butter

(4 servings)

BASIL BUTTER

15	fresh basil leaves	15
3	garlic cloves, peeled	3
¼ tsp	cayenne pepper	1 mL
¼ lb	unsalted butter	125 g
	few drops lemon juice	
	salt and white pepper	

SALMON

4	salmon steaks	4
¼ lb	basil butter	125 g
8	tomato slices	8
4	lemon slices	4
4	bay leaves	4
	salt, pepper and paprika	

- To make basil butter, mix basil and garlic together in the bowl of a food processor. Add remaining ingredients and season to taste. Mix again until well combined.
- Preheat barbecue to medium.
- Place each salmon steak on a double piece of aluminum foil. Place a spoonful of basil butter on each steak and top with two slices of tomato. Add a lemon slice and a bay leaf. Season and seal packages.
- Place foil packages on grill. Cover and cook 25 to 30 minutes.

●

Note: If desired, the salmon can be cooked in a 325°F (160°C) oven.

1 SERVING			
Calories	493	Carbohydrate	3 g
Protein	40 g	Fat	36 g
Fiber	1.4 g		

Salmon Fillets with Maître d'Hôtel Butter

(4 servings)

MAÎTRE D'HÔTEL BUTTER

½ lb	butter, softened	250 g
2 tbsp	chopped fresh parsley	30 mL
1 tsp	finely chopped chives	5 mL
	juice of ½ lemon	
	few drops of Worcestershire sauce	
	few drops of Tabasco sauce	
	salt and pepper	

FILLETS

4	salmon fillets	4
1 cup	seasoned flour	250 mL
2 tbsp	butter	30 mL
1 tsp	vegetable oil	5 mL
4	slices maître d'hôtel butter	4
	juice of 1 lemon	
	salt and pepper	

- Mix butter ingredients together in food processor. Place a sheet of aluminum foil on counter. Spoon butter along center of foil and roll into a cylinder. Twist ends shut.
- Preheat oven to 375°F (190°C).
- Season fish and dredge in flour; set aside.
- Heat 2 tbsp (30 mL) butter with oil in a frying pan over medium heat. When hot, add fillets and cook 6 to 8 minutes depending on thickness. Turn fish over 3 to 4 times during cooking.
- Sprinkle fish with lemon juice, transfer to oven and finish cooking, about 6 minutes. When done, place a slice of maître d'hôtel butter on each fillet and serve.

●

Note: This butter will keep 3 months in the freezer.

1 SERVING			
Calories	434	Carbohydrate	14 g
Protein	41 g	Fat	24 g
Fiber	0 g		

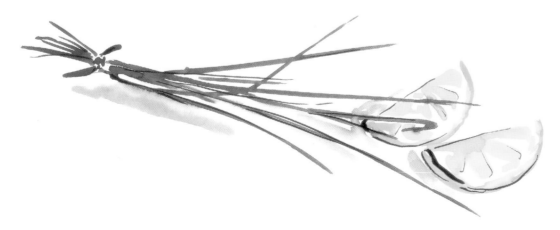

Salmon Steaks with Pesto

(4 servings)

4	small salmon steaks	4
½ cup	chopped fresh basil	125 mL
2	garlic cloves, blanched, peeled and smashed	2
3 tbsp	grated Parmesan cheese	45 mL
3 tbsp	olive oil	45 mL
	few drops of lemon juice	
	salt and pepper	
	oil	

- Brush salmon steaks with oil and place on platter. Season with salt and pepper and sprinkle with lemon juice. Set aside.

- Place basil and garlic in food processor; process 10 seconds.

- Add cheese and replace top. Add oil gradually while mixing. Continue mixing until oil is well incorporated. Season to taste. Set pesto aside.

- Heat a cast-iron pan over medium heat. When pan is hot, add oiled salmon steaks. Cook 12 minutes, turning fish over 2 to 3 times during cooking.

- When salmon is cooked, serve with pesto. Accompany with lemon slices and vegetables.

1 SERVING			
Calories	365	Carbohydrate	1 g
Protein	41 g	Fat	22 g
Fiber	0 g		

Vegetable Stock

1 tsp	butter	5 mL
1	onion, sliced	1
1	large carrot, sliced	1
½	celery rib, sliced	½
1	shallot, finely chopped	1
3	parsley sprigs	3
¼ tsp	fennel seed	1 mL
¼ tsp	tarragon	1 mL
6 cups	water	1.5 L
	salt and pepper	

- To prepare vegetable stock, heat butter in a large saucepan over medium heat. Add vegetables and seasonings. Cover and cook 5 minutes over low heat.
- Stir in water and season well. Bring to a boil and cook 20 minutes over low heat.
- Strain liquid and set aside.

Poached Salmon Steaks with Cucumber

(4 servings)

4	salmon steaks, ¾-inch (2 cm) thick	4
1	large cucumber	1
5 cups	vegetable stock, heated	1.25 L
1 tsp	chopped fresh parsley	5 mL
	lemon wedges	
	salt and pepper	

- Place salmon steaks in a sauté pan. Set aside.
- Peel cucumber and cut in half lengthwise. Seed and slice.
- Cover salmon steaks with sliced cucumber. Season with salt and pepper and pour in vegetable stock. Place on stove over medium heat and bring to a boil. Reduce heat to low and simmer 5 minutes.
- Remove salmon from liquid and place on serving platter. Garnish with cucumber and sprinkle with parsley.
- Serve with fresh lemon.

1 SERVING			
Calories	306	Carbohydrate	9 g
Protein	41 g	Fat	12 g
Fiber	1.2 g		

Salmon Steaks with Dill Hollandaise

(4 servings)

4	salmon steaks	4
1 tbsp	melted butter	15 mL
1½ tsp	lemon juice	7 mL
1 tsp	olive oil	5 mL
2 tbsp	chopped fresh dill	30 mL
1 cup	Hollandaise sauce (see page 252)	250 mL
	salt and pepper	

- Season salmon steaks.
- Mix butter with 1 tsp (5 mL) lemon juice. Brush mixture over both sides of each salmon steak.
- Heat oil in a cast-iron pan over medium heat. Add salmon steaks and cook 12 minutes. Turn salmon over 3 to 4 times during cooking and season with salt and pepper.
- Stir fresh dill and remaining lemon juice into Hollandaise sauce.
- Serve salmon with the sauce.

1 SERVING			
Calories	342	Carbohydrate	4 g
Protein	41 g	Fat	18 g
Fiber	0 g		

Pan-Fried Salmon Trout Fillets

(4 servings)

1 tbsp	olive oil	15 mL
1 tsp	butter	5 mL
4	salmon trout fillets	4
⅓ cup	pine nuts	75 mL
1 tbsp	chopped fresh parsley	15 mL
	juice of 1 lemon	
	salt and pepper	

- Heat oil and butter in a frying pan over medium heat. Add fillets and cook 4 minutes.
- Turn fillets over and season well. Continue cooking about 3 minutes, depending on thickness of fillets. Remove fish from pan and keep hot.
- Add pine nuts and parsley to frying pan; cook 1 minute. Add lemon juice and season with pepper; cook 20 seconds.
- Pour juices over hot fish. Serve with sautéed potatoes.

1 SERVING

Calories	346	Carbohydrate	2 g
Protein	23 g	Fat	28 g
Fiber	0 g		

Whole Trout with Green Grapes

(4 servings)

4	small whole trout, cleaned	4
1 cup	all-purpose flour	250 mL
2 tbsp	olive oil	30 mL
2 tbsp	butter	30 mL
2	shallots, chopped	2
1½ lb	seedless green grapes	750 g
1	lemon, peeled, seeded and diced	1
1 tbsp	chopped fresh parsley	15 mL
	salt and pepper	

- Preheat oven to 400°F (200°C). Season cavities of fish and dredge in flour.
- Heat oil in a large ovenproof frying pan over medium heat. Add fish and cook 2 minutes on each side.
- Transfer frying pan to oven and cook fish 8 minutes, or according to size. When done, transfer fish to serving platter and tent with foil.
- Return pan with juices from fish to stove over medium heat. Add butter and remaining ingredients; sauté 2 minutes. Correct seasoning and pour over trout. Serve.

1 SERVING			
Calories	617	Carbohydrate	56 g
Protein	42 g	Fat	25 g
Fiber	2.8 g		

Sautéed Halibut Steaks

(4 servings)

4	halibut steaks	4
1 cup	seasoned flour	250 mL
2 tbsp	butter	30 mL
1 tbsp	vegetable oil	15 mL
1	carrot, thinly sliced	1
1	green pepper, thinly sliced	1
1	celery rib, thinly sliced	1
1 cup	fish stock, heated	250 mL
½ tsp	cornstarch	2 mL
2 tbsp	cold water	30 mL
	salt and pepper	
	lemon juice	

- Season fish and dredge in flour. Heat butter and oil in a large ovenproof frying pan over medium heat. Add halibut and cook about 8 minutes; adjust time depending on thickness of steaks. Turn fish over 2 to 3 times during cooking.

- Transfer pan to oven and finish cooking fish 6 minutes. Remove fish from pan to serving platter and keep warm.

- Add all vegetables to frying pan and season well. Cover and cook 4 minutes over medium heat.

- Pour in fish stock and bring to a boil. Cook 1 minute.

- Dissolve cornstarch in cold water; stir into vegetable mixture until well blended. Cook 1 minute over reduced heat.

- Spoon vegetables beside fish, sprinkle with lemon juice and serve at once.

1 SERVING

Calories	325	Carbohydrate	16 g
Protein	34 g	Fat	14 g
Fiber	1 g		

Barbecued Sweet and Sour Halibut

(4 servings)

4	halibut steaks, about 6 oz (175 g) each	4
3 tbsp	peanut oil	45 mL
1 tbsp	sesame oil	15 mL
2 tbsp	soy sauce	30 mL
2 tbsp	honey	30 mL
3	garlic cloves, finely chopped	3
¼ cup	chicken stock	50 mL
	juice of ½ lemon	
	freshly ground pepper	

- Place halibut steaks in a roasting pan and season with pepper. In a bowl, mix together peanut oil, sesame oil, soy sauce, honey, garlic, chicken stock and lemon juice.
- Pour mixture over fish and marinate 1 hour. Turn steaks over and marinate 1 hour or more.
- Grill fish on preheated barbecue 6 to 7 minutes on each side, or adjust time depending on thickness. Baste frequently during cooking.
- Serve fish with vegetable rice and zucchini, if desired.

●

Note: Soy sauce is made from a fermented mixture of soy beans, salt, ground wheat and yeast. Light soy sauce is used as a seasoning; it is a bit saltier and enhances fish especially well. The darker version is made with molasses and is aged longer. Used in cooking, it has a stronger flavor.

1 SERVING			
Calories	358	Carbphydrate	11 g
Protein	38 g	Fat	18 g
Fiber	0.1 g		

Halibut Steaks with Bell Peppers and Red Onion

(4 servings)

4	halibut steaks, rinsed and dried	4
½ cup	all-purpose flour	125 mL
3 tbsp	olive oil	45 mL
1	small red onion, thinly sliced	1
1	red pepper, thinly sliced	1
1	yellow pepper, thinly sliced	1
2	garlic cloves, sliced	2
1 tbsp	chopped fresh ginger	15 mL
1 tbsp	soy sauce	15 mL
	salt and pepper	
	lemon juice	

- Season halibut generously with salt and pepper. Dredge in flour.
- Heat 2 tbsp (30 mL) oil in a large frying pan over high heat. Add fish and reduce heat to medium. Cook 3 minutes. Turn halibut over and cook 3 minutes more.
- Turn fish over again and cook 2 minutes, or according to size. When fully cooked, remove from pan and keep warm in oven.
- Add remaining oil to hot pan. Add all remaining ingredients, except soy sauce and lemon juice, and cook 5 minutes over high heat. Stir occasionally.
- Sprinkle in soy sauce and lemon juice, to taste. Stir, pour over fish and serve.

1 SERVING			
Calories	371	Carbohydrate	17 g
Protein	42 g	Fat	15 g
Fiber	1.4 g		

Halibut and Potato Casserole

(4 servings)

3	halibut steaks, rinsed	3
½ cup	dry white wine	125 mL
2	shallots, chopped	2
1	fresh thyme sprig	1
2	fresh fennel sprigs	2
2	fresh parsley sprigs	2
2½ cups	water	625 mL
32	raw parisienne potatoes	32
32	fresh mushroom caps, cleaned	32
2	carrots, pared and cut in small sticks	2
3 tbsp	butter	45 mL
3 tbsp	all-purpose flour	45 mL
	salt and pepper	

- Place fish in a large sauté pan. Add wine, shallots and herbs. Cover with water and season well. Bring to a boil over medium heat.

- As soon as the water comes to a boil, reduce heat to low. Turn fish over and simmer 3 minutes. Remove fish from pan and set aside.

- Add potatoes, mushrooms and carrots to liquid remaining in pan. Cover and cook until tender. Remove vegetables and set aside. Discard herbs and reserve cooking liquid.

- Heat butter in a saucepan over medium heat. Sprinkle in flour and mix well. Cook 1 minute.

- Incorporate 2 cups (500 mL) of cooking liquid from fish. Season generously and cook sauce 6 minutes to thicken.

- Bone and flake fish. Arrange in a baking dish and cover with vegetables. Pour sauce over top and broil in oven until heated through. Serve.

1 SERVING			
Calories	386	Carbohydrate	32 g
Protein	35 g	Fat	12 g
Fiber	3.6 g		

Sole Fillets in Cream Sauce

(4 servings)

4	large sole fillets	4
¼ cup	dry white wine	50 mL
1	red pepper, cut in strips	1
1	green pepper, cut in strips	1
½ tsp	curry powder	2 mL
¼ cup	heavy cream	50 mL
	juice of 1 lime	
	salt and pepper	

- Place fillets in a large buttered frying pan. Season with salt and pepper.
- Add wine, lime juice and peppers. Cover with a sheet of waxed paper, laid on the surface of the food. Bring to a boil over medium heat.
- As soon as liquid starts to boil, remove pan from heat. Let stand 2 minutes.
- Remove fish and vegetables from pan; keep hot.
- Return pan to stove over high heat. Incorporate curry powder into liquid and cook 3 minutes.
- Stir in heavy cream and continue cooking 3 minutes over high heat.
- Pour sauce over fillets and serve.

1 SERVING

Calories	188	Carbohydrate	3 g
Protein	18 g	Fat	10 g
Fiber	0 g		

*F*illet of Sole Amandine

(4 servings)

4	large sole fillets	4
1 cup	all-purpose flour	250 mL
2 tbsp	butter	30 mL
1 tsp	vegetable oil	5 mL
3 tbsp	slivered almonds	45 mL
1 tbsp	chopped fresh parsley	15 mL
	salt and pepper	
	paprika	
	juice of 1 lemon	

- Season fillets with salt, pepper and paprika. Dredge in flour.
- Heat butter and oil in a large frying pan over high heat. Add fish and cook 2 minutes. Turn fillets over and continue cooking 2 minutes. Transfer fish to a heated serving platter.
- Add almonds, parsley and lemon juice to frying pan; cook 1 minute over high heat. Spoon over sole and serve at once.

1 SERVING			
Calories	264	Carbohydrate	15 g
Protein	20 g	Fat	14 g
Fiber	1 g		

Fresh Fillet of Sole with Mushrooms

(4 servings)

4	fresh sole fillets	4
½ cup	all-purpose flour	125 mL
2 tbsp	olive oil	30 mL
1 tbsp	butter	15 mL
½ lb	fresh mushrooms, cleaned and sliced	250 g
1 tbsp	chopped fresh parsley	15 mL
	salt and pepper	
	juice of 1 lemon	

- Season fillets generously with salt and pepper, and dredge in flour.

- Heat oil in a frying pan over high heat. Add sole and cook 2 minutes. Turn fillets over and cook 1 minute.

- Transfer fillets to ovenproof platter and keep warm in oven.

- Add butter to hot frying pan. Add mushrooms and season well; cook 4 minutes over high heat. Add parsley and lemon juice, stir and pour over fillets. Serve immediately.

1 SERVING			
Calories	315	Carbohydrate	16 g
Protein	38 g	Fat	11 g
Fiber	2 g		

Turbot with Sun-Dried Tomatoes

(4 servings)

2	large turbot fillets, halved	2
2	shallots, chopped	2
1	celery rib with leaves, sliced	1
1 cup	dry white wine	250 mL
1½ cups	water	375 mL
2	fresh fennel sprigs	2
1	fresh thyme sprig	1
2	fresh parsley sprigs	2
1 tbsp	olive oil	15 mL
3	garlic cloves, smashed and chopped	3
3	tomatoes, peeled, seeded and chopped	3
2 tbsp	chopped sun-dried tomatoes	30 mL
1 tbsp	chopped fresh basil	15 mL
	salt and pepper	
	lemon juice	

- Arrange fillets in a large frying pan. Add shallots, celery, wine, water and fresh herb sprigs. Season well and cover with a sheet of waxed paper, laid on the surface of the food. Bring to a boil over medium heat.

- Reduce heat to low and turn fillets over. Simmer 2 minutes. Remove fish and set aside.

- Heat cooking liquid over high heat until reduced by one third; set aside.

- Heat oil in another frying pan over high heat. Add garlic and cook 1 minute. Add fresh and sun-dried tomatoes. Sprinkle in basil and season well. Cook 6 minutes over high heat.

- Add fish and some of the reserved cooking liquid to tomato mixture. Simmer 3 minutes to reheat turbot. Sprinkle with lemon juice and serve.

1 SERVING			
Calories	261	Carbohydrate	7 g
Protein	33 g	Fat	9 g
Fiber	1.4 g		

Turbot au Gratin

(4 servings)

4	turbot fillets	4
2	shallots, chopped	2
½ lb	fresh mushrooms, cleaned and quartered	250 g
1 cup	dry white wine	250 mL
1 cup	cold water	250 mL
1	fresh fennel sprig	1
2 tbsp	butter	30 mL
2 tbsp	all-purpose flour	30 mL
1 tbsp	chopped fresh parsley	15 mL
1 cup	grated Gruyère cheese	250 mL
	salt and pepper	

- Season fillets generously on both sides. Place in a sauté pan with shallots, mushrooms, wine, water and fennel sprig. Season well and cover with a sheet of waxed paper, laid on the surface of the food. Bring to a boil over medium heat.

- Reduce heat to low and simmer 2 minutes. Remove fillets from pan and keep warm in oven. Continue cooking liquid in pan 6 minutes over high heat.

- Heat butter in another saucepan over medium heat. Sprinkle in flour, mix well and cook 30 seconds. Incorporate reduced cooking liquid and mushrooms. Simmer 8 minutes over low heat and correct seasoning.

- Arrange fish in a baking dish and cover with sauce. Sprinkle with parsley and top with cheese. Broil 3 minutes or until golden brown, and serve.

1 SERVING			
Calories	532	Carbohydrate	70 g
Protein	7 g	Fat	24 g
Fiber	1.6 g		

Fillet of Flounder with Oyster Sauce

(4 servings)

½ tsp	white pepper	2 mL
½ tsp	black pepper	2 mL
¼ tsp	dry mustard	1 mL
¼ tsp	cayenne pepper	1 mL
½ tsp	celery seed	2 mL
¼ tsp	ground ginger	1 mL
1 cup	all-purpose flour	250 mL
4	flounder fillets	4
1 cup	milk	250 mL
3 tbsp	butter	45 mL
1½ cups	oyster sauce, heated (see page 251)	375 mL

- Grind spices together with a mortar and pestle. Mix flour with spices.
- Dip fillets in milk, then dredge in spiced flour.
- Heat butter in a cast-iron pan over medium heat. Add fillets and cook 3 minutes on each side. Remove fish and serve with oyster sauce.

1 SERVING			
Calories	547	Carbohydrate	39 g
Protein	30 g	Fat	30 g
Fiber	1.6 g		

Monkfish with Tomato Basil Coulis

(4 servings)

2 tbsp	olive oil	30 mL
1	onion, finely chopped	1
1	garlic clove, smashed and chopped	1
4	large tomatoes, cored and cut in six	4
3 tbsp	chopped fresh basil	45 mL
¼ cup	fish stock (see page 18)	50 mL
2 tbsp	tomato paste	30 mL
4	medium monkfish fillets	4
	pinch brown sugar	
	salt and pepper	

- Preheat oven to 350°F (180°C).

- Heat 1 tbsp (15 mL) olive oil in a sauté pan over medium heat. Add onion and garlic; cook 6 minutes over low heat.

- Add tomatoes and basil. Season and cook 10 minutes over low heat, stirring occasionally.

- Stir in fish stock, tomato paste and brown sugar. Continue cooking 6 to 7 minutes.

- Heat remaining oil in another frying pan over medium heat. Add fish and cook 2 minutes on each side.

- Transfer fish to a roasting pan and top with tomato mixture. Cook in oven 10 minutes or adjust time according to size of fillets.

●

Note: For a creamier sauce, strain tomato sauce through a sieve and stir in 2 tbsp (30 mL) sour cream before serving.

1 SERVING			
Calories	342	Carbohydrate	9 g
Protein	42 g	Fat	15 g
Fiber	2 g		

Grouper Burgers

(4 servings)

4	small pieces grouper, about ¼ lb (125 g) each	4
1	garlic clove, smashed and chopped	1
3 tbsp	Chinese black bean sauce	45 mL
4	onion buns	4
4	large slices mozzarella cheese	4
	few drops of Worcestershire sauce	
	juice of 1 lemon	
	lettuce leaves, washed and dried	
	salt and pepper	

- Place grouper on a large plate.
- Mix garlic, bean sauce, Worcestershire sauce and lemon juice together in a small bowl. Pour sauce over fish and marinate 10 minutes.
- Preheat oven to broil.
- Slice onion buns open and place under broiler. Brown 2 minutes, then remove and keep hot.
- Remove fish from marinade and arrange in a roasting pan. Place under broiler and cook 3 minutes on each side.
- Remove fish from oven; skin and debone. Place a piece of fish on each bun and brush with remaining marinade. Season with salt and pepper.
- Top fish with cheese and place in middle of oven. Broil 2 minutes.
- Add lettuce leaves and replace tops of buns. Serve with tomatoes and potato chips.

1 SERVING

Calories	486	Carbohydrate	32 g
Protein	49 g	Fat	18 g
Fiber	1.7 g		

Grouper Braised in Tomatoes

(4 servings)

1 tbsp	olive oil	15 mL
2	small onions, sliced	2
1	garlic clove, smashed and chopped	1
4	small tomatoes, peeled, cored and quartered	4
4 tsp	Dijon mustard	20 mL
4	grouper steaks	4
1 cup	fish stock, heated (see page 182)	250 mL
¼ tsp	fennel seed	1 mL
	salt and pepper	

- Preheat oven to 425°F (220°C).

- Heat oil in a frying pan over medium heat. Add onions and garlic; cook 5 minutes. Stir once during cooking.

- Add tomatoes and season well. Cover and continue cooking 5 minutes.

- Spread mustard over grouper steaks. Place fish in ovenproof baking dish and cover with tomato mixture. Pour in fish stock and sprinkle with fennel seed.

- Cook 10 to 12 minutes in oven or adjust cooking time according to size of grouper steaks.

1 SERVING			
Calories	280	Carbohydrate	9 g
Protein	37 g	Fat	11 g
Fiber	2.4 g		

Cod with Tomato Fondue

(4 to 6 servings)

TOMATO FONDUE

1 tbsp	olive oil	15 mL
1	onion, chopped	1
1	celery rib, diced	1
3	garlic cloves, smashed and chopped	3
1	28-oz (796 mL) can tomatoes, drained and chopped, or 4 large tomatoes, peeled and chopped	1
1 tsp	basil	5 mL
½ tsp	thyme	2 mL
¼ tsp	cayenne pepper	1 mL

COD

1	celery rib, diced	1
1	carrot, diced	1
1	onion, diced	1
3	parsley sprigs	3
2	bay leaves	2
4 cups	water	1 L
2 lb	fresh cod, cut in four pieces	900 g
2 cups	tomato fondue	500 mL

- For the fondue, heat oil in a saucepan over medium heat. Add onion, celery, and garlic. Cook 6 minutes over low heat.
- Add remaining fondue ingredients and mix well. Bring to a boil over medium heat. Reduce heat to low and continue cooking 18 minutes. Set aside.
- Preheat oven to 350°F (180°C).
- Place vegetables and seasonings in roasting pan. Pour in water and bring to a boil over high heat.
- Add fish and cook 6 minutes over low heat. The fish should be covered completely by the liquid.
- Remove the fish from the liquid and drain well. Transfer to buttered ovenproof baking dish; season well. Cover with tomato fondue and place in oven. Bake 6 minutes. Serve.

1 SERVING

Calories	361	Carbohydrate	9 g
Protein	53 g	Fat	13 g
Fiber	2.4 g		

Cod with Mashed Potatoes and Swiss Cheese

(4 servings)

1 tbsp	butter	15 mL
1½ lb	fresh cod fillets, rinsed	750 g
3	shallots, peeled and chopped	3
1	fresh thyme sprig	1
2	fresh parsley sprigs	2
4	potatoes, peeled and thinly sliced	4
¼ cup	grated Swiss cheese	50 mL
	salt and pepper	

• Grease a baking dish with butter and set aside. Place cod in a large saucepan and season generously. Add shallots, fresh herbs and potatoes.

• Cover with cold water. Bring to a boil over medium heat. Reduce heat to low and simmer 3 minutes.

• Remove fish and set aside; discard herbs. Continue cooking potatoes until tender.

• Remove potatoes from dish, drain well and pass through food mill.

• Place cod in the greased baking dish and top with puréed potatoes. Season well with pepper and sprinkle with grated Swiss cheese. Broil 5 minutes or until lightly browned. Serve.

1 SERVING			
Calories	289	Carbohydrate	20 g
Protein	41 g	Fat	5 g
Fiber	1.8 g		

Hearty Cod Stew

(4 servings)

4	bacon slices, diced	4
½	red onion, chopped	½
2	garlic cloves, smashed and chopped	2
4	potatoes, peeled and diced	4
4 cups	vegetable stock, heated	1 L
2	fresh fennel sprigs	2
1½ lb	fresh cod, rinsed and cubed	750 g
2 tbsp	butter	30 mL
2 tbsp	all-purpose flour	30 mL
1 tbsp	chopped fresh parsley	15 mL
	salt and pepper	

• Cook bacon 6 minutes in a large saucepan over medium heat. Add onion and garlic. Reduce heat to low and cook 4 minutes.

• Stir in potatoes, vegetable stock and fresh fennel. Season well and cook 12 minutes over low heat.

• Add fish and cook 6 minutes. Discard fennel sprigs. Remove 1 cup (250 mL) of cooking liquid and set aside.

• Heat butter in another saucepan over medium heat. Sprinkle in flour and mix well. Cook 15 seconds. Incorporate reserved cooking liquid. Pour mixture into pan containing fish and vegetables; mix gently. Add parsley and serve.

1 SERVING			
Calories	403	Carbohydrate	30 g
Protein	46 g	Fat	11 g
Fiber	3.2 g		

Pickerel with Fresh Herbs

(4 servings)

4	pickerel fillets, rinsed and dried	4
2 tbsp	olive oil	30 mL
2 tbsp	butter	30 mL
1 tbsp	chopped fresh parsley	15 mL
1 tbsp	chopped fresh chives	15 mL
1 tbsp	chopped fresh tarragon	15 mL
	salt and pepper	
	juice of 1 lemon	

- Season fillets generously with salt and pepper. Heat oil in a frying pan over high heat. Add fish and reduce heat to medium. Cook 3 minutes.

- Turn fillets over and continue cooking 2 minutes. Fish is cooked when flesh feels firm to the touch. Do not overcook. Transfer fillets to serving platter.
- Add butter to pan and increase heat to high. Add herbs and lemon juice. Mix and cook 10 seconds.
- Pour over fish and serve immediately.

1 SERVING			
Calories	197	Carbohydrate	1 g
Protein	19 g	Fat	13 g
Fiber	0 g		

Fresh Cod with Tomato Curry

(4 servings)

2 tbsp	olive oil	30 mL
1	Spanish onion, peeled and thinly sliced	1
2 tbsp	curry powder	30 mL
12	cherry tomatoes, halved	12
2 lb	fresh cod fillets, rinsed	1 kg
1 cup	clam juice	250 mL
1 cup	water	250 mL
1	fresh thyme sprig	1
1	fresh fennel sprig	1
1	fresh parsley sprig	1
1 tbsp	cornstarch	15 mL
2 tbsp	cold water	30 mL
	salt and pepper	
	juice of 1 lemon	

- Heat oil in a sauté pan over medium heat. Add onion and cook 6 minutes over low heat, stirring occasionally.

- Sprinkle in curry powder and mix well. Continue cooking 3 minutes.
- Stir in cherry tomatoes and season well. Cook 4 minutes.
- Add fish, clam juice, water and fresh herbs. Season well and bring to a boil over medium heat.
- As soon as liquid boils, reduce heat to low. Turn fish over and simmer 3 minutes or until done. Remove fish from pan and keep warm in oven.
- Dilute cornstarch in cold water. Incorporate to sauce and cook 4 minutes over high heat. Pour over fish, sprinkle with lemon juice and serve.

1 SERVING			
Calories	349	Carbohydrate	19 g
Protein	48 g	Fat	9 g
Fiber	1.6 g		

Baked Pickerel

(4 servings)

4	medium pickerel fillets	4
1 tbsp	chopped fresh parsley	15 mL
2	large tomatoes, cored and sliced thick	2
2	fennel sprigs	2
2	tarragon sprigs	2
¼ cup	dry white wine	50 mL
3	garlic cloves, smashed and chopped	3
4 tsp	butter	20 mL
	salt and pepper	

- Preheat oven to 375°F (190°C).
- Place fish, skin-side down, in roasting pan. Season with salt and pepper; sprinkle with parsley.
- Arrange tomato slices on fillets. Add fresh herbs. Pour in wine and add garlic.
- Place a nob of butter on each fillet. Bake 15 minutes in oven. Serve.

1 SERVING

Calories	144	Carbohydrate	4 g
Protein	20 g	Fat	5 g
Fiber	1 g		

Broiled Pickerel

(4 servings)

¼ tsp	crushed bay leaves	1 mL
¼ tsp	black pepper	1 mL
¼ tsp	paprika	1 mL
¼ tsp	celery seed	1 mL
2 tbsp	olive oil	30 mL
4	medium pickerel fillets	4
	juice of 2 limes	
	salt	

- Preheat oven to broil.
- Grind all the spices together with a mortar and pestle. Add oil and lime juice; mix together.
- Brush mixture over both sides of fillets.
- Place fillets, skin-side down, on ovenproof platter. Place in oven, 6 inches (15 cm) from broiler element, and broil 7 to 8 minutes. Do not turn fish over.
- Serve with vegetables.

1 SERVING

Calories	154	Carbohydrate	2 g
Protein	19 g	Fat	8 g
Fiber	0 g		

Sautéed Pickerel Fillets with Anchovy Butter

(4 servings)

ANCHOVY BUTTER		
2½ oz	anchovy fillets	70 g
½ lb	unsalted butter, at room temperature	250 g
1 tsp	chopped chervil	5 mL
	juice of ¼ lemon	
	pinch of cayenne pepper	
	few drops Tabasco sauce	
	salt and pepper	

FILLETS		
2 tbsp	olive oil	30 mL
4	pickerel fillets, rinsed and dried	4
	salt and pepper	

- Purée anchovy fillets with a mortar and pestle and push through a fine-meshed sieve into a clean bowl.
- Add remaining anchovy butter ingredients to anchovy purée. Mix well and correct seasoning.
- Roll anchovy butter in foil and seal ends tightly. Refrigerate until needed or freeze for up to 3 months.
- Heat oil in a frying pan over medium heat. Season fillets generously and add to pan. Cook 3 minutes. Turn fish over and cook 3 to 4 minutes, or according to size.
- Transfer cooked fish to ovenproof platter and keep warm in oven. Serve with anchovy butter.

●

Note: If you don't have a mortar and pestle, chop the anchovies twice and push through fine-meshed sieve.

1 SERVING			
Calories	367	Carbohydrate	0 g
Protein	22 g	Fat	31 g
Fiber	0 g		

Whole Snapper with Spring Vegetables

(4 servings)

¼ tsp	oregano	1 mL
¼ tsp	cumin	1 mL
2	garlic cloves, smashed and chopped	2
1	4–5 lb (1.8–2.5 kg) whole red snapper, prepared for cooking	1
5	fresh fennel sprigs	5
4 tbsp	olive oil	60 mL
12	baby carrots	12
2	bunches green onions, cut in 1-inch (2.5 cm) lengths	2
½ cup	dry white wine	125 mL
	salt and pepper	
	juice of 4 limes	

- Preheat oven to 400°F (200°C). Mix oregano, cumin, garlic, salt and pepper together. Sprinkle in cavity of fish. Stuff fish with fennel sprigs and add half of lime juice.

- Place fish in a baking dish. Drizzle with 2 tbsp (30 mL) oil and remaining lime juice. Season generously, cover with plastic wrap and chill 30 minutes.

- Pour remaining oil over snapper and surround with baby carrots. Cook 35 minutes in oven.

- Add green onions and cook 6 more minutes in oven, or until fish is cooked.

- Transfer fish to serving platter.

- Place baking dish on stove over medium heat. Add wine and cook 3 minutes. Pour over fish and serve.

1 SERVING			
Calories	578	Carbohydrate	7 g
Protein	90 g	Fat	20 g
Fiber	1.2 g		

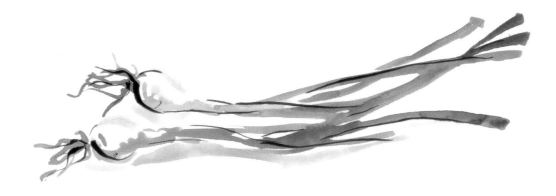

Red Snapper with Roasted Pecans

(4 servings)

¼ tsp	black pepper	1 mL
¼ tsp	paprika	1 mL
½ tsp	fennel seed	2 mL
4	large red snapper fillets	4
3 tbsp	butter	45 mL
⅓ cup	roasted pecans	75 mL
1 tbsp	chopped fresh parsley	15 mL
	lemon juice	
	salt	

- Grind pepper, salt, paprika and fennel seed together with a mortar and pestle. Sprinkle mixture over both sides of each fillet.
- Heat 2 tbsp (30 mL) butter in a large frying pan over medium heat. Add fish and cook 4 minutes.
- Turn fillets over and continue cooking 3 to 4 minutes or adjust cooking time according to size of fillets. Remove cooked fillets from pan and keep hot.
- Add remaining butter to pan and melt. Add pecans and cook 1 minute. Add lemon juice and mix. Pour over fish, sprinkle with parsley and serve.

1 SERVING

Calories	282	Carbohydrate	6 g
Protein	19 g	Fat	20 g
Fiber	0 g		

Red Snapper Cooked in Foil

(4 servings)

2	2 lb (1 kg) whole red snappers, prepared for cooking	2
4 tbsp	butter	60 mL
1	bunch fresh fennel	1
1	bunch fresh parsley	1
2	bay leaves	2
2	garlic cloves, chopped	2
2 tbsp	olive oil	30 mL
½ cup	dry white wine	125 mL
	salt and pepper	
	lime juice to taste	
	lemon juice to taste	

- Preheat oven to 450°F (230°C).

- Season fish inside and out. Divide butter, lime juice, herbs, bay leaves and garlic between cavities. Truss fish and baste skins with oil. Season well.

- Place each fish in a large piece of doubled foil. Add wine and fold package to secure juices. Place in a roasting pan and cook in oven.

- Fillet fish and serve with cooking juices and lemon juice.

1 SERVING			
Calories	377	Carbohydrate	10 g
Protein	35 g	Fat	20 g
Fiber	0.6 g		

Grilled Whole Mackerel with Herb Butter Sauce

(4 servings)

FISH

2	2 lb (1 kg) fresh whole mackerels, prepared for cooking	2
2 tbsp	butter	30 mL
1	bunch fresh fennel	1
1	bunch fresh flat-leaf parsley	1
2	bay leaves	2
2	garlic cloves, chopped	2
¼ cup	olive oil	50 mL
	salt and pepper	
	juice of 1 lemon	

HERB BUTTER SAUCE

3 tbsp	butter	45 mL
2	shallots, chopped	2
1 tbsp	chopped fresh parsley	15 mL
1 tsp	chopped fresh tarragon	5 mL
	pepper	
	juice of 1½ lemons	

- Season fish inside and out. Divide butter, lemon juice, herbs, bay leaves and garlic between cavities. Truss fish and baste skins with oil. Season well.

- Grill fish 7 to 8 minutes over hot coals. Baste with olive oil during cooking. Adjust time according to size; do not overcook. When done, flesh will feel firm to the touch and central bone will turn white.

- Meanwhile, make sauce. Heat butter in a small saucepan over medium heat. Add shallots, herbs and pepper. Cook 20 seconds.

- Add lemon juice, pour over fish and serve.

●

Note: Choosing and handling fresh fish requires some care. When buying whole fish, look for clear, bright eyes and firm flesh. Cook fresh fish within 1 day of purchase. Pack on ice and rinse well before cooking.

1 SERVING			
Calories	581	Carbohydrate	3 g
Protein	41 g	Fat	45 g
Fiber	0.6 g		

Baked Swordfish with Almonds

(4 servings)

4	small swordfish steaks, rinsed and dried	4
2 tbsp	olive oil	30 mL
1 tbsp	butter	15 mL
¼ cup	slivered almonds	50 mL
2 tbsp	capers	30 mL
1 tbsp	chopped fresh parsley	15 mL
	salt and pepper	
	juice of 2 limes	

- Preheat oven to 375°F (190°C). Season fish with salt and pepper.
- Heat oil in a large, ovenproof frying pan over medium heat. Add fish and cook 2 minutes. Turn fish over and cook 1 minute.
- Transfer pan to oven and cook 6 to 7 minutes, or according to size. When cooked, transfer fish to serving platter and keep warm in oven.
- Return frying pan with juices from fish to stove over medium heat. Add butter, almonds, capers and parsley; cook 2 minutes.
- Add lime juice, pour over fish and serve.

1 SERVING			
Calories	283	Carbohydrate	3 g
Protein	25 g	Fat	19 g
Fiber	0.6 g		

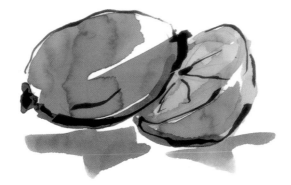

Cajun Butter

(8 to 10 servings)

¼ tsp	black pepper	1 mL
¼ tsp	white pepper	1 mL
¼ tsp	sage	1 mL
1 tsp	minced jalapeño pepper	5 mL
2	garlic cloves, blanched, peeled and puréed	2
½ lb	unsalted butter, soft	250 g
	pinch cayenne pepper	
	juice of ½ lemon	
	salt	

- Mix spices, jalapeño pepper and garlic together in a bowl. Add butter and mix until well incorporated. Season with salt and lemon juice. Mix again.
- Transfer butter to a large sheet of aluminum foil. Shape butter into a cylinder, roll foil and twist ends shut. Freeze and use as needed.

1 SERVING

Calories	206	Carbohydrate	0 g
Protein	0 g	Fat	23 g
Fiber	0 g		

Broiled Swordfish

(4 servings)

4	swordfish steaks	4
1 tbsp	olive oil	15 mL
4	slices Cajun butter	4
	lemon juice	
	salt and pepper	

- Preheat oven to broil.
- Brush both sides of each swordfish steak with oil. Place in oven and broil 4 minutes on each side. The time may vary depending on the thickness of the steaks. Season during cooking.
- To serve, place a slice of Cajun butter on each hot swordfish steak and sprinkle with lemon juice.

1 SERVING

Calories	317	Carbohydrate	0 g
Protein	41 g	Fat	17 g
Fiber	0 g		

Hot Chili Pepper Butter

(8 to 10 servings)

½ lb	salted butter, softened	250 g
2	roasted chili peppers, puréed	2
3	garlic cloves, blanched, peeled and puréed	3
1 tbsp	chopped fresh chives	15 mL
¼ tsp	cayenne pepper	1 mL
	juice of ½ lemon	

- Place all ingredients in bowl of food processor; blend until well mixed.
- Transfer butter to a large sheet of aluminum foil. Shape butter into a cylinder and roll in foil. Twist ends shut and store in freezer.

Note: This butter will keep 3 months in freezer. Each time you wish to use some, simply open package and cut off desired number of slices. Always roll tightly in foil and twist ends shut.

1 SERVING

Calories	205	Carbohydrate	1 g
Protein	1 g	Fat	22 g
Fiber	0 g		

Creamy Fish Sauce

4 tbsp	unsalted butter	60 mL
4 tbsp	all-purpose flour	60 mL
3 cups	fish stock, heated	750 mL
	salt and pepper	

- Melt butter in a saucepan over medium heat. Stir in flour and cook 1 minute over low heat. Pour in stock, season and mix well. Cook over low heat until sauce becomes thick and creamy.

2 tbsp (30 mL)

Calories	114	Carbohydrate	5 g
Protein	1 g	Fat	10 g
Fiber	0.2 g		

*O*yster Sauce

(4 to 6 servings)

1 cup	shucked oysters with their juice	250 mL
2½ cups	cold water	625 mL
¼ tsp	black pepper	1 mL
¼ tsp	white pepper	1 mL
¼ tsp	ground basil	1 mL
1	garlic clove, blanched, peeled and puréed	1
3 tbsp	butter	45 mL
1	onion, chopped	1
3 tbsp	all-purpose flour	45 mL
¼ cup	heavy cream	50 mL
	pinch nutmeg	
	pinch cayenne pepper	
	salt	

- Pour oysters with their juice in a bowl. Add cold water and refrigerate 8 hours.
- Drain oysters and pour liquid into a small saucepan, reserving oysters. Bring to a gentle boil; cook 3 to 4 minutes over low heat.
- Mix peppers and basil with garlic; set aside.
- Heat butter in another saucepan or cast iron pan. Add onion and cook 4 minutes over low heat. Add flour, mix and cook 1 minute over low heat.
- Gradually incorporate liquid from oysters; whisk constantly. Add spice mixture and heavy cream. Mix well and cook 12 minutes over low heat, stirring frequently. The sauce should become quite thick. If desired, add oysters to sauce and simmer 3 minutes. Serve with a variety of dishes.

1 SERVING			
Calories	149	Carbohydrate	7 g
Protein	5 g	Fat	11 g
Fiber	0 g		

*B*asil Butter

(4 to 6 servings)

½ lb	unsalted butter, softened	250 g
15	fresh basil leaves, chopped	15
1 tbsp	chopped fresh parsley	15 mL
1	shallot, chopped	1
¼ tsp	pepper	1 mL
¼ tsp	paprika	1 mL
	few drops Tabasco sauce	
	few drops lemon juice	

- Place all ingredients in bowl of food processor. Blend until combined.
- Transfer butter to a large sheet of aluminum foil. Shape butter into a cylindrical tube, roll foil and twist ends shut. Freeze.
- Use as needed.

1 SERVING			
Calories	375	Carbohydrate	2 g
Protein	1 g	Fat	40 g
Fiber	0 g		

Beurre Blanc

½ lb	cold unsalted butter	250 g
2	shallots, chopped	2
	juice of 1 lime	
	salt and pepper	

2 tbsp (30 mL)

Calories	45	Carbohydrate	0 g
Protein	0 g	Fat	5 g
Fiber	0 g		

- Melt 1 tbsp (15 mL) of butter in a saucepan and sauté shallots 2 minutes. Add lime juice and simmer to thicken. Add the rest of the butter, bit by bit, whisking constantly over low heat. Season with salt and pepper. The sauce should become creamy.
- Keep warm over low heat until ready to use. If necessary, whisk lightly just before serving.

Hollandaise Sauce

2	egg yolks	2
1 tbsp	cold water	15 mL
¾ cup	melted clarified butter	175 mL
	lemon juice	
	salt and pepper	

2 tbsp (30 mL)

Calories	22	Carbohydrate	0 g
Protein	1 g	Fat	25 g
Fiber	0 g		

- Beat egg yolks with water in a stainless steel bowl. Season with salt and pepper and place bowl over a saucepan of simmering water.
- Add butter bit by bit, whisking constantly, until sauce is thick and creamy. Add lemon juice to taste and correct seasoning.

Tartar Sauce

1	recipe mayonnaise (see page 82)	1
1	shallot, chopped	1
1 tbsp	chopped fresh parsley	15 mL
2 tbsp	chopped fresh chives	30 mL
2 tbsp	chopped capers	30 mL
4 tbsp	chopped dill pickle	60 mL
	pepper	

- Mix all ingredients together and refrigerate until ready to use.

2 tbsp (30 mL)

Calories	157	Carbohydrate	1 g
Protein	0 g	Fat	17 g
Fiber	0.1 g		

Cocktail Sauce

1	recipe mayonnaise (see page 250)	1
6 tbsp	chili sauce	90 mL
2 tbsp	horseradish	30 mL
2 tbsp	lemon juice	30 mL
	salt and pepper	

• Combine mayonnaise, chili sauce and horseradish; mix well. Add lemon juice and season with salt and pepper. Chill before serving.

2 tbsp (30 mL)			
Calories	160	Carbohydrate	3 g
Protein	1 g	Fat	16 g
Fiber	0.6 g		

Fine Herb Coulis

4 tbsp	chopped fresh dill	60 mL
½ cup	chopped fresh chives	125 mL
½ cup	chopped fresh parsley	125 mL
½ cup	chopped fresh chervil	125 mL
1 cup	chicken stock, heated	250 mL
3 tbsp	extra virgin olive oil	45 mL
	salt and pepper	

• Place dill, chives, parsley, chervil and chicken stock in blender or food processor and purée.
• Gradually add olive oil in a thin stream and continue blending. Season and serve hot or at room temperature.

2 tbsp (30 mL)			
Calories	44	Carbohydrate	1 g
Protein	1 g	Fat	4 g
Fiber	0 g		

Basil Oil

2 cups	olive oil	500 mL
2 cups	fresh basil leaves	500 mL

• Pour olive oil into a blender or food processor; add basil and purée. Transfer to a glass or ceramic jar and let stand 24 hours.
• Strain, making sure to recuperate as much oil as possible, and keep in a cool place until ready to use. This oil is wonderful with salads and grilled fish.

2 tbsp (30 mL)			
Calories	252	Carbohydrate	0 g
Protein	0 g	Fat	28 g
Fiber	0 g		

INDEX